"Melissa Bahen has created a completely hygge world in this book."

—ADRIANNA ADARME,
author of *The Year of Cozy*

"*Scandinavian Gatherings* in one word: nostalgia! It is just the book I would have loved to have had when I moved to Scandinavia myself."

—BRITTANY JEPSEN,
TheHouseThatLarsBuilt.com

"*Scandinavian Gatherings* is full of the kind of sweet celebrations that make the world a more magical and meaningful place."

—JENNIFER SHEA, author of
Trophy Cupcakes & Parties!

"Melissa Bahen has captured everything I love about the culture that I married into—including delicious, comforting baked goods and whimsical, timeless decor rooted in folk tradition. This book will make decorating and cooking for your gatherings just as fun as the gatherings themselves!"

—MOLLY YEH, MyNameIsYeh.com

"[The] go-to guide for a Scandinavian gathering."

—425 MAGAZINE

"A delightful book packed with mouthwatering recipes and charming craft ideas, perfect for anyone looking for a hands-on way to re-create traditional Scandinavian festivities, alone or with the help of the entire family."

—NIKI BRANTMARK,
MyScandinavianHome.com

"I'd like to escape into the pages of *Scandinavian Gatherings* every afternoon, exactly when only a Cream Cake with Fresh Strawberries or Waffle Cookies will do. This gem of a cookbook mixed with crafty projects inspires me to make and celebrate."

—MAGGIE BATTISTA, author of *Food Gift Love* and founder of Eat Boutique

"A collection of seasonal entertaining, craft and food projects drawing from Scandinavian style and traditions."

—OREGON PUBLIC BROADCASTING

"Really lovely. . . gorgeous photography. If you're into the Scandinavian lifestyle, which I know everybody is, this is a great one!"

—DESIGN MOM

Scandinavian
GATHERINGS

FROM AFTERNOON FIKA TO CHRISTMAS EVE SUPPER
70 Simple Recipes for Year-Round Hygge

MELISSA BAHEN

Photographs by Charity Burggraaf • Illustrations by Andrea Smith

SASQUATCH BOOKS
SEATTLE

✦›)))❂(((‹• ✦›)))❂(((‹• ✦›)))❂(((‹•

This book is dedicated to my family—to my husband and children, my parents, and my siblings. And to my nana and poppy, who have always fostered a deep love of my Scandinavian heritage. *Tack så mycket!*

✦›)))❂(((‹• ✦›)))❂(((‹• ✦›)))❂(((‹•

Contents

•))⟩❂⟨⟨• •))⟩❂⟨⟨• •))⟩❂⟨⟨•

Recipes & Projects

❖⟩⟩⟩❂⟨⟨⟨❖ ❖⟩⟩⟩❂⟨⟨⟨❖ ❖⟩⟩⟩❂⟨⟨⟨❖

HERITAGE DINNER

LUCIA DAY

CHRISTMAS COOKIE EXCHANGE

CHRISTMAS EVE SUPPER

BIRTHDAY TREATS

Foreword

+}}·❂·{{(• •}}·❂·{{(• •}}·❂·{{(•

AS SOMEONE WHO WAS BORN and raised in Norway, I am often asked the question, "What's different about Scandinavian food?" I always give the same answer: "The winter!" There, the days are dark and very cold, so what else is there to do other than eat and drink?

My fondest childhood memories include my *mormor* (*grandmother* in Norwegian), who would cook and bake all winter long. Every fall she and my great-aunt would make jam, chutney, and *saft* (a drink made from berry concentrate mixed with water). As a matter a fact my entire family had to leave the house for a week while they were preserving the summer harvest so we wouldn't get in their way. My parents were okay with it, as we all went to Spain and had fun. I still remember returning from our trips to find the house smelling sweet from all the preserving they'd done. Mormor would proudly show me the basement with all the shelves filled up with jars—she called them her "jars of sunshine"—and in the middle of winter she would ask us to go down to the basement and get her a jar of sunshine. I still call raspberry jam that to this day.

Whether you have Scandinavian heritage or simply an interest in our food and culture, I think you'll enjoy this book. *Scandinavian Gatherings* is a lovely collection of recipes and craft projects inspired by Nordic holidays and celebrations. Many of these gatherings evoke memories from my childhood, and they are a fun introduction to the traditions both Melissa and I grew up with. Scandinavian food is simple, easy, and has a deep respect for the ingredients. But you don't have to have grown up in Scandinavia to enjoy the seasonal celebrations and foods, because now you have Melissa's book to explore.

Happy cooking!

—PAUL LOWE, founder and EIC of *Sweet Paul Magazine*

Introduction

•}}}❂{{{• •}}}❂{{{• •}}}❂{{{•

FOR AS LONG AS I CAN REMEMBER, I have loved to make things, both in the kitchen and out of it. I take after my mom in that respect; she has always been enormously creative, whether she was tole painting decorative plates when I was a child or carefully illustrating a church newsletter. Her talents extend into the kitchen as well. She and her mother, Nana, are both amazing cooks, and my family has always been very big on traditions, especially those that involve food. Growing up, we ate Sunday dinner together every week at the dining room table, either at our house or at Nana's—and we still have regular Sunday dinners together! Nana taught us early how to set a proper table, and we were excited when it was our turn to help because we got to select the dishes, the tablecloth, the centerpiece, and the candlesticks. My family loves getting together for holidays too, and our traditions are deeply ingrained in us. We eat the same foods and do the same activities on the same holidays every year, whether we are gathered together to celebrate at my parents' house or spread out across the country.

Being surrounded by delicious food and comforting traditions when I was a child set me on a course early in life that has led me to write this book. When I was young, my cousin and I decided to start a catering company when we grew up, and we spent the summer mailing our favorite recipes to each other. In high school I started keeping a binder full of recipes that I had torn out of magazines. I still have it on my cookbook shelf. There's a little gold-star sticker next to each recipe that I tried and loved, and a few of the really memorable ones are still in regular rotation. In between college semesters one year, I was in charge of my family's dinner menu for the entire summer. I think my mom paid me fifty dollars for all that work! I still have the piece of scratch paper that I wrote menu ideas on.

This book marries my longtime love of cooking and making with my beloved Norwegian heritage. My mom's dad, Poppy, was born in 1929 to Axel and Asta Andresen, Norwegian immigrants who had settled in Utah's Salt Lake Valley. Poppy spent his childhood speaking Norwegian and developing a love for pickled herring and open-faced sandwiches. While he didn't pass on a love for pickled herring to his children and grandchildren, he did pass on a deep and abiding love for our Scandinavian heritage.

Sadly, very few of the traditional Norwegian recipes my poppy grew up with were passed down to subsequent generations. One of the most wonderful things about writing this book has been not only rediscovering and falling in love with classic Scandinavian foods, but also recreating some of the delicious recipes I've heard so much about in family lore. I'm excited to bring these lost treasures back to my family. I hope my children have fond memories of making Tante Tilda's Norwegian Silver-Dollar Pancakes (page 4) with me the way my mom remembers making them with Tante Tilda. I want my children to carry on the tradition of serving Rødgrød med Flød (Raspberry Pudding with Cream), page 167, on Christmas Eve like they have for dessert every year at Nana and Poppy's house.

Each chapter of this book will give you ideas for creating a complete gathering, a get-together of family and dear friends. I love that word: *gathering*. A gathering is comfortable and easy, almost effortless, intimate, full of good food and the best company. A gathering isn't as stuffy or as formal as a party; it's both coolly casual and supremely sophisticated. Along with the recipes and craft projects in each chapter, you'll find ideas for styling, serving, arranging, and more. But feel free to add your special touch to these gatherings and make them your own.

If you have Scandinavian heritage like me, I hope you'll be delighted to find old favorites alongside new recipes inspired by the flavors and traditions of the region. But even if you have no connection to Scandinavia, I have a feeling that some of these are destined to become family favorites just the same. Cookies for a school bake sale, open-faced sandwiches for a light lunch, cake for a friend's birthday dinner—all of the recipes are as delicious on a regular weeknight as they are at a festive gathering. The Nordic-inspired projects in each chapter are perfect for holidays and festive occasions, but they also make for a fun crafting afternoon with friends or great rainy-day projects with kids.

I've loved every step of this journey taking *Scandinavian Gatherings* from a daydream to a beautiful reality. I'm thrilled with the results—the recipes, the projects, the colorful artwork—and can't wait to share my beloved heritage with you!

Norwegian Sea

SWEDEN

NORWAY

FINLAND

Helsinki

Gulf of Bothnia

North Sea

Oslo

Gulf of Finland

Stockholm

Baltic
Sea

DENMARK

Copenhagen

N
W · E
S

What Is Scandinavia?

•}}}⊕{{{• •}}}⊕{{{• •}}}⊕{{{•

TECHNICALLY, JUST DENMARK, NORWAY, AND SWEDEN are part of the Scandinavian region. But the true answer isn't quite as simple as that. Norway, Sweden, and Finland— and not Denmark—are part of the Scandinavian Peninsula, the actual geographic fingers of land that extend into the ocean from the northernmost part of Europe. Because of cultural similarities, proximity, language, history, and more, Finland is closely associated with the Scandinavian countries, and often included unofficially, especially by us Americans. It happens often enough that there's an actual term for adding Finland to Scandinavia: *Fenno-Scandinavia*. In these pages you'll find recipes and projects inspired by all four countries: *rosemåling*, the traditional folk painting of Norway; flower crowns worn by girls during Swedish Midsummer festivities; the candy-colored houses of Danish harbor towns; and the cardamom-scented baked goods of Finland.

About Ingredients & Techniques

❖})}❖{((• ❖})}❖{((• ❖})}❖{((•

FLOUR

UNLESS OTHERWISE NOTED, flour is always all-purpose flour. And I always fork sift my flour before measuring it. Just stir the flour with a fork, using a fluffing/stirring motion, until the flour feels light and the fork moves through it smoothly and without meeting resistance. To measure the flour, dip your measuring cup in so that it is much fuller than it needs to be, then use the flat side of a butter knife to scrape the extra flour off the top. Don't shake the extra flour off, because then you'll undo all of that fluffy fork sifting you worked so hard on!

BUTTER

UNLESS OTHERWISE NOTED, butter is salted butter. I know lots of cookbooks call for unsalted butter, and if you want to use it, you can. I just happen to have regular salted butter on hand all the time—it's one of our staples—and find that most people I've talked to do as well. So that's what I used when creating these recipes. If you are worried about the freshness of your butter (which is one of the main reasons cookbooks often call for unsalted butter), go buy a new box of salted butter and check the expiration date on the package to make sure it is fresh.

HERBS

A GENERAL RULE OF THUMB for substituting dried herbs for fresh herbs in cooking is to use one-third the amount. So if a recipe calls for one tablespoon of a chopped fresh herb, you can use one teaspoon of the same herb dried.

YEAST

YEAST BREADS CAN SEEM INTIMIDATING, but I've figured out a way to have success with them every time: I proof my yeast in a hot water bath. After combining the yeast and a pinch of sugar with the warm water (or milk or buttermilk) as directed by the recipe, run your tap water as hot as it will go, and fill a medium bowl with about two inches of hot water. Set the measuring cup with the yeast mixture in it in the bowl of hot water (making sure the hot water is nowhere near the edge of the glass measuring cup) and watch the magic happen. You'll know everything is working if there are bubbles and the mixture has increased significantly in volume after five minutes. If it still seems sluggish, dump the hot water out of the medium bowl, refill it with fresh hot water, and try again. This method has never failed me, and it can be used with all of the yeast bread recipes in this book.

Nordic
Brunch

EVERY SUMMER, MY MOM'S FAMILY gets together for a big family reunion
we like to call Rammfest. It's named after my grandpa, Poppy, whose full
name is Bruce Ramm Andresen. A wonderfully Norwegian name, isn't it?
For years, though, apart from its name and the occasional Norwegian flag
draped from a flagpole, Rammfest wasn't a terribly Scandinavian event.
But one year, we thought it would be fun to celebrate our Nordic heritage,
so we planned a full day of meals and activities inspired by Scandinavia.
We ate Swedish meatballs and cream cake and little jars of pickled herring
(although I'm pretty sure Poppy is the only one who enjoyed that last one).
We set up an enormous flower-covered maypole on the lawn, and even
surprised my grandparents by dressing up in makeshift *bunads* (traditional
Norwegian folk costumes) and parading into my aunt and uncle's backyard,
all fifty-something of us!

My aunt's breakfast casserole is an old family recipe that served as the
inspiration for this gathering when it made its revamped Scandinavian
debut at Rammfest that summer. Other recipes are longtime family breakfast favorites with a Nordic touch.

CREATING THE GATHERING

A breakfast feast should be light and bright. I have an old tablecloth I bought at a secondhand store that looks like it belongs in a Swedish farmhouse—a white cloth with a sunny-yellow border and a scattering of colorful flowers across the center. If you have cheerful old-fashioned table linens, a Scandinavian brunch is the perfect place to use them, and if not, a plain white tablecloth is always a safe choice. Blossoms arranged in a tall white milk pitcher or a few small bouquets of wildflowers in little jars make sweet additions to the table. And don't forget the beverages! A selection of juices and teas will round out the menu nicely, along with every Scandinavian's favorite—coffee!

RECIPES

Tante Tilda's Norwegian Silver-Dollar Pancakes
Mom's Maple Pecan Rings
Ham, Havarti & Chive Breakfast Casserole
Homemade Honey-Almond Granola with Yogurt & Fresh Berries

PROJECTS

Stenciled Swedish Dala Horse Napkins
Danish Townhouse Place Card Holders
Rustic Welcome Sign

TANTE TILDA'S NORWEGIAN SILVER-DOLLAR PANCAKES

•⟫⟩⟩❂⟨⟨⟨• •⟫⟩⟩❂⟨⟨⟨• •⟫⟩⟩❂⟨⟨⟨•

My great-grandmother Asta passed away when my grandpa was a teenager, so my mom and her siblings never knew her. But Asta's oldest sister, Mathilde, who had helped raise Asta and all of her siblings in Norway, took a job as a cook in a mansion in downtown Salt Lake City to be near her family. Tante Tilda, as she was called, became a surrogate grandmother to my mom's family. They would go visit her at work, and she would let them help her make her famous pancakes.

I've heard about Tante Tilda's pancakes my whole life; they're a bit of a legend. My mom and her sisters remember standing on a kitchen chair next to Tante Tilda while she dropped tablespoonfuls of batter onto a hot, buttered skillet to make silver-dollar pancakes. They were topped with piping hot maple syrup that had a big pat of salty butter melted into it.

MAKES 4½ DOZEN 3-INCH PANCAKES

Maple syrup, for serving
Butter
1½ cups plus
    2 tablespoons flour
1 tablespoon sugar
½ teaspoon table salt
2 cups whole milk
2 eggs

Special equipment:
Large nonstick or cast-
    iron skillet

1. In a small saucepan over low heat, heat the maple syrup. Add a pat of butter and allow it to melt into the syrup while making the pancakes. Keep the syrup over low heat until the pancakes are ready to be served.

2. Heat a large nonstick or cast-iron skillet over medium to medium-low heat.

3. In a large bowl, whisk together the flour, sugar, and salt. In a large glass measuring cup, whisk together the milk and eggs. Pour the wet ingredients into the dry ingredients, and whisk until smooth.

4. Place a thin pat of butter on the hot skillet, allow it to melt and bubble, and spread it around with the edge of a spatula.

5. Working in batches, scoop the batter by the tablespoonful onto the skillet. Cook the pancakes for 30 seconds, or until they are golden on the bottom. Flip and cook them for 30 seconds more. If the pancakes don't turn golden after 30 seconds, increase the heat. If the pan starts to smoke or the butter begins to turn dark brown, reduce the heat slightly, wipe the pan out with a paper towel, and add a new pat of butter.

6. Serve the pancakes hot with the buttered maple syrup.

MOM'S MAPLE PECAN RINGS

•∙}}}❂{{{∙• •∙}}}❂{{{∙• •∙}}}❂{{{∙•

These pastries are one of my family's most prized treats. My mom has been making them for over three decades, ever since she got the recipe from her sister-in-law, who got it from a friend who owned a bakery. When we were growing up, my siblings and I would fight over who got the piece in the center. It always ends up with the most cinnamon-sugar filling, the most sweet icing, and the most gooey dough—the best part of an already amazing treat. If you are lucky enough to get a pan of warm pecan rings from my mom, it's a sure sign that she likes you. With their intricate shape and delicious maple flavor, pecan rings are the perfect pastry to make when you want to impress.

1. In a small saucepan, combine the milk and sugar; whisk until the sugar is dissolved. Add the butter and heat over medium low, stirring gently, until the butter is melted. Remove from the heat and set aside.

2. In a glass measuring cup or small bowl, combine the yeast, warm water, and a pinch of sugar. Allow the mixture to sit for 5 minutes to make sure yeast is active and alive. You should see bubbles on the surface, and the mixture should grow in volume (see page xix for tips on making yeast breads).

3. In a large bowl with a wooden spoon or in the bowl of a stand mixer fitted with the paddle attachment, add the milk mixture and the yeast mixture. Add the salt, eggs, and 7 cups of the flour. Mix until combined. The dough will still be very sticky, and that's okay.

4. Transfer the dough to a very large, lightly oiled bowl, cover with oiled plastic wrap, and let it rise in a warm spot until doubled in size, about 1 hour.

5. While the dough is rising, make the filling. In a small bowl, combine the pecans, sugar, cinnamon, and maple. Stir with a fork until well mixed; set aside.

MAKES 34 PASTRIES

2 cups whole milk
½ cup sugar, plus a pinch
    for proofing the yeast
1 cup butter
3 tablespoons active
    dry yeast
⅔ cup warm water
1½ teaspoons table salt
2 eggs
8½ cups flour, divided

For the filling:
2 cups chopped pecans
1½ cups sugar
3 teaspoons ground
    cinnamon
3 teaspoons maple
    extract or
    maple flavoring
¼ cup butter, melted

CONTINUED

For the icing:
2 cups confectioners'
   sugar
3 tablespoons whole milk
1 capful natural lemon
   extract (about
   ½ teaspoon)

Special equipment:
2 (12-inch) circular pans,
   such as pizza pans
3-inch round biscuit
   cutter

If you don't have a 3-inch round biscuit cutter or cookie cutter, you can do what my mom does—use the ring from a mason jar lid. My mom always has a few canning rings in her cookie cutter drawer just for making pecan rings!

6. Punch down the risen dough, add the remaining 1½ cups flour, and knead by hand for 1 to 2 minutes on a well-floured surface.

7. Divide the dough into six equal portions (each pan of pecan rings will have three layers of dough). Roll out one portion of dough into a 12-inch circle and place it on a lightly oiled 12-inch pizza pan. Brush the entire surface with melted butter, then top with one-sixth of the filling mixture (about a couple of spoonfuls). Roll out another portion of dough into a 12-inch circle, place it on top of the first, brush with butter, and top with more filling. Repeat with one more portion of dough, topping it with the melted butter and filling mixture. Make sure to get the butter and filling mixture all the way to the edges. Repeat step 7 with the remaining three portions of dough and another 12-inch pizza pan.

8. Use a 3-inch biscuit cutter to cut a circle in the center of each pecan ring. Use a clean pair of kitchen shears or scissors to cut the rest of the dough into sixteen wedges, cutting all the way from the outside edge, through all three layers of filling and dough, until you reach the center portion. Stop just short of that center circle. (I cut mine in half first, then cut each half in half again, then each quarter in half again, and so on until I have sixteen equal pieces.)

9. Gently pick up the outside edge of each wedge and give it one and one half complete twists. You should end up with the bottom on the top at the outside edge. After twisting, firmly press the edge back onto the pan. Repeat with the other fifteen wedges, then repeat with the other pan.

10. Lightly cover the pecan rings and allow them to rise for 30 minutes more.

11. Preheat the oven to 375 degrees F. Bake the pecan rings for 18 to 20 minutes, or until golden.

12. While the pecan rings bake, make the icing. In a small bowl, whisk together the confectioners' sugar, milk, and lemon extract. When the pecan rings come out of the oven, drizzle the icing over the warm pastries. Allow them to cool slightly before serving. They are best eaten the day they are made, but leftovers taste especially good when reheated for a few seconds in the microwave.

step 8

step 9a

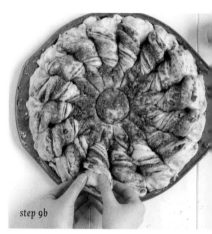

step 9b

Hotels across Scandinavia have the most spectacular breakfast buffets I've ever seen. They usually have a variety of sliced breads, deli meats and cheeses, yogurts, fresh fruits and vegetables, cereal, and caviar. Yes, caviar! Scandinavian breakfast buffets are always stocked with caviar packaged in individual-size tubes that look strangely like toothpaste.

HAM, HAVARTI & CHIVE BREAKFAST CASSEROLE

•}}}❂{{{• •}}}❂{{{• •}}}❂{{{•

This savory breakfast casserole is an old family recipe, but it only recently got a Scandinavian makeover. My Aunt Shelly introduced our family to it when I was in elementary school. Ever since then, we've made it often for family get-togethers because it is such a crowd-pleaser. A few years ago, my mom tweaked the original recipe for the Norwegian-themed breakfast at our family reunion, and it was a huge hit. Salty ham, fresh chives, and mild Danish cheese give this easy-to-prepare breakfast bake a Scandinavian twist.

**MAKES 12 TO
16 SERVINGS**

16 eggs
⅜ teaspoon table salt
1 small clove garlic, finely
   minced, or ⅛ teaspoon
   garlic powder
Pinch of freshly ground
   black pepper
2 cups whole milk
12 ounces ham, diced
   (no larger than ¼-inch
   squares)
2 cups shredded Havarti
   cheese
2 cups shredded cheddar
   cheese
⅓ cup snipped fresh
   chives, divided

1. Preheat the oven to 375 degrees F and lightly spray a 9-by-13-inch baking pan with nonstick cooking spray.

2. In a large bowl, beat the eggs with a whisk until uniform. Beat in the salt, garlic, and pepper, then beat in the milk. Stir in the ham, cheeses, and two-thirds of the chives with a rubber spatula. Pour the mixture into the prepared pan, using the rubber spatula to scrape the bowl as necessary and then evenly distribute the ham, cheese, and chives if needed.

3. Bake the casserole for 45 minutes, or until a knife inserted in the center comes out wet but clear, and the top of the casserole is deeply golden.

4. Allow the casserole to cool for 5 to 10 minutes before serving. Serve topped with the remaining chives.

Havarti is a softer cheese than cheddar. Try putting it in the freezer for 15 minutes immediately before shredding it to make it easier to work with.

HOMEMADE HONEY-ALMOND GRANOLA WITH YOGURT & FRESH BERRIES

Muesli—a mixture of raw oats, seeds, nuts, and dried fruits—is hugely popular all over Europe, including in Scandinavian countries. Every hotel I remember staying at in Sweden and Norway had a huge complimentary breakfast buffet, and the buffets always included muesli. Muesli doesn't have a huge following here in the United States, but its lightly sweetened and toasted cousin, granola, is a perennial favorite, and it's so simple to make at home. I love to eat it by the handful as a snack, and it's my favorite breakfast, especially when topped with honey-flavored Greek yogurt and fresh summer strawberries.

MAKES ABOUT 6 CUPS

- 3 cups rolled oats
- 1 cup shelled raw pumpkin seeds
- 1 cup shelled raw sunflower seeds
- 1 cup sliced raw almonds
- ½ cup lightly packed light brown sugar
- ¾ cup honey
- ½ cup extra-virgin olive oil
- 1 teaspoon table salt
- 1 cup dried sour cherries or other dried fruits (optional)
- Yogurt, for serving
- Fresh berries, for serving

Special equipment:
Parchment paper

1. Preheat the oven to 300 degrees F and spray a baking sheet with nonstick cooking spray.

2. In a large bowl, combine the oats, pumpkin seeds, sunflower seeds, almonds, and brown sugar.

3. In a glass measuring cup, combine the honey, oil, and salt. Microwave the measuring cup for 30 seconds, stir briefly, and then pour the wet ingredients over the oat mixture. Stir until everything is evenly coated. Spread the granola out on the prepared baking sheet, and bake for 45 minutes, stirring every 15 minutes, or until the granola is golden.

4. While the granola is baking, place a piece of parchment paper on a clean baking sheet, and set aside.

5. Remove the granola from the oven and immediately scrape it onto the parchment-lined baking sheet. Spread it out and let it cool. It will be very sticky when it first comes out of the oven, but it will crisp up as it cools.

6. When the granola is completely cool, crumble it into small chunks with your hands, and then mix in the cherries. Serve with the yogurt and berries. Store leftovers in an airtight container for up to 10 days.

STENCILED SWEDISH DALA HORSE NAPKINS

•)))✺(((• •)))✺(((• •)))✺(((•

Dala horses, whose bright orangey-red color and whimsical detailing have become national symbols of Sweden, are named for the Swedish province of Dalarna where they originated. One of my favorite crafting techniques is freezer-paper stenciling. Freezer paper is very inexpensive and available at most grocery stores, and with just a little patience makes fantastic stencils. It's perfect for painting designs onto fabric, such as these dala horse napkins.

1. Turn to the dala horse template. Trace the dala horse design onto freezer paper with a pencil; trace one horse for each napkin you want to make. Be sure to trace onto the rough, papery side, not the shiny side, and leave at least 4 inches between each horse.

2. Cut the traced dala horses apart, leaving lots of freezer paper around each design. Then carefully cut out the inside of each design. Keep in mind while cutting that you are creating a stencil. The piece of freezer paper that you are cutting the dala horse out of is the part you'll be keeping. The design itself will be thrown away.

3. Lay out the napkins flat on the ironing board, making sure the design is in the desired position. I positioned my dala horse stencils in the lower-left corner of each napkin so that when the napkins are folded in eighths, the design is still visible. If you make a mistake on this step, you'll have to start over. Freezer paper stencils can only be ironed once, so take your time when placing the stencil on the napkin. With the iron set to the cotton setting and the steam turned off, iron the freezer paper onto the napkin, shiny side down. The heat from the iron will melt the plastic enough to make it stick to the fabric, but when you're finished, it will pull off very easily. Pay special attention to the inside edges of the design, making sure they are completely smooth.

MATERIALS & TOOLS:

Stenciled Swedish Dala Horse Napkins template (page 212)

Freezer paper

Pencil

Narrow-tipped scissors

Plain white cloth napkins, washed, dried, and pressed

Ironing board

Iron

Fabric paint in red, white, pink, yellow, and light blue (see page 208 for exact colors)

Paper plate, cardboard, or something to put the paint on

Sponge brush

Clean rag or pressing cloth

CONTINUED

4. Squeeze a small amount of paint onto a paper plate, then carefully use the sponge brush to apply paint to the exposed area of the napkin. Use a dabbing motion as opposed to big brushstrokes, and try to smooth out any big globs of paint.

5. As soon as a design is filled in, remove the freezer paper and set the napkin aside in a safe place to dry.

6. Once the bottom layer of paint is dry, use pink, yellow, or light-blue paint and a fine-tipped paintbrush to add a mane and a saddle to each dala horse, as seen in the photo (see page 12). Use white paint and the blunt end of the paintbrush to add white dots for the bridle, cinch, reins, etc.

7. Allow the painted napkins to dry completely, then cover them with a clean rag or pressing cloth, and iron over the painted areas to set the paint. Launder gently.

DANISH TOWNHOUSE PLACE CARD HOLDERS

⚬⟩⟩⟩❋⟨⟨⟨⚬ ⚬⟩⟩⟩❋⟨⟨⟨⚬ ⚬⟩⟩⟩❋⟨⟨⟨⚬

Nyhavn, or "New Harbor" in Danish, is a waterfront area in Copenhagen that is famous for its colorful buildings. Yellow, orange, blue, red, and pink, the white-trimmed houses are one of the most famous sights in Denmark—just ask any postcard! These adorable little townhouse card holders are so versatile. They can hold place cards at a breakfast gathering, menu cards at a dinner party, and even photos, postcards, and keepsakes.

1. At the hardware store, have them cut your 2-by-2-inch piece of wood into 6-inch sections.

2. Use the handsaw to cut each section of wood in half. There's no real need to measure here, because the goal is to get blocks of slightly different heights—just eyeball it! Try to make your cuts as straight as possible; if you have one, a miter box will help. The ends that were cut at the hardware store will be perfectly straight; make those ends the bottoms of the houses, and the cuts you make can be the tops.

3. Make a straight cut about ¼ inch deep across the square face of each block that will be the roof. This will be the slot for place cards.

4. Sand all of the cut edges of each block with the sandpaper until they are smooth. Tuck the sandpaper down into the card slot and sand both sides of that lightly as well.

5. Using a sponge brush, paint each block, starting with the color for the main part of the house (white, orange, red, yellow, pink, or light blue). You don't need to paint the top or bottom of the block, just the four sides. Paint as many coats as needed, allowing each coat to dry before adding another.

MATERIALS & TOOLS:

1 (2-by-2-inch) piece of wood

Small handsaw or jigsaw

Miter box (optional)

Sandpaper

Sponge brush

Craft paint in white, red, dark gray, terra-cotta, pastel pink, pastel blue, pastel yellow, and pale orange (see page 208 for exact colors)

Painter's tape

Soft-bristled paintbrush, about ¼ inch wide

White fine-tipped oil-based paint marker

CONTINUED

6. Next, tape off the roofline using the painter's tape. Some roofs can run side to side (with the peak on the front of the house) and some can run the opposite direction (with the peaks on the sides of the house). Mix it up for some variety! Paint the roofs in either dark gray or terra-cotta. Make sure to paint the top of each block as well. Paint as many coats as needed. As soon as you are done painting, remove the tape and allow the roofs to dry.

7. Use the soft-bristled brush to paint a few dark-gray windows on the front of the house. The windows don't need to look like perfect little rectangles; using a single stroke of the brush for each window is fine. Don't worry about a door, or windows on the sides or back of the house. Let the paint dry completely.

8. Using the white paint marker, draw a line between the house and the roof to represent the white trim work common on Nyhavn houses. Draw white trim around the windows too, and draw a cross on each window to create windowpanes.

9. Allow the paint to dry completely. If the slot for the cards has paint stuck in it, gently pop your handsaw back into the space to dislodge any paint and to reopen the slot.

step 6

You can find the wood for this project in the lumber department of your local hardware store. Clear cedar is a great choice. It is soft, so it is easy to cut with a handsaw, and it doesn't have any knots.

RUSTIC WELCOME SIGN

•)))◑(((• •)))◑(((• •)))◑(((•

Beautifully painted welcome signs are popular in the friendly region of Scandinavia. My grandparents have had a Norwegian welcome sign on every house they've ever lived in. This rustic plaque is a simple, modern version of the classic *velkommen* sign. It looks just as cute hanging on a cozy kitchen wall as it does on a front door.

MATERIALS & TOOLS:

Large tree trunk slice, about 1 inch thick and about 10 inches wide

Soft-bristled paintbrush, about 1 inch wide

Clear liquid acrylic sealer

Light-blue acrylic craft paint (see page 208 for exact color)

Photocopier or scanner/printer

Rustic Welcome Sign template (page 213)

Plain white paper

Scissors

Pencil

Red fine-tipped oil-based paint marker

2 small eye screws

18 inches (¼-inch-wide) red grosgrain ribbon

1. Find the side of the tree trunk slice with fewer knots. This will be the front of your plaque. Use the paintbrush to paint a large oval on the tree trunk slice with clear acrylic sealer. This will keep any knots or imperfections in the wood from bleeding through the paint. Keep the sealer 1 inch away from the edge of the wood. Allow the sealer to dry, then paint over the exact same area with light-blue paint. You will need to paint two to three coats to get a nice opaque layer. Allow each coat to dry completely before moving on.

2. While the paint is drying, photocopy the welcome sign template onto a plain white sheet of paper. Trim the paper so that it is just larger than the text. Hold the paper up to a bright window so that the blank side is facing you, and make a sesame seed–size dot with the pencil at the center of each *X*.

3. Lay the sheet of paper pencil side down on the dry plaque so that the writing is centered top to bottom and left to right. Scribble over the whole word with a pencil, pressing very firmly. When you remove the paper, the pencil dots from the back of the paper should have transferred to the painted plaque.

4. Use the red paint marker to make a small *X* on top of each pencil dot. Follow the welcome sign template if you get lost. Allow the paint marker to dry completely before moving on.

5. When the paint marker is dry, attach both eye screws to the plaque, one about 4 inches left of the center, one about 4 inches to the right. To attach the screws, hold the plaque firmly with one hand while pushing a screw in firmly with the other hand. Start by just pushing the screw in while twisting it back and forth until you've made a small divot in the surface of the wood. Then screw it in with full turns until it is tight.

6. Knot one end of the ribbon through the hole in one eye screw, and knot the other end through the hole in the other eye screw.

HERE'S HOW TO SAY *WELCOME* IN SCANDINAVIA:

Norway: *Velkommen*

Sweden: *Välkommen*

Denmark: *Velkommen*

Finland: *Tervetuloa*

Woodland Tea Party

THERE'S SOMETHING MAGICAL ABOUT SCANDINAVIA, from the brightly painted homes lining the harbor in Denmark to the northern lights that dance across the summer sky near the Arctic Circle. It's a region tailor-made for stories, legends, and fairy tales. My grandparents lived in Sweden for several years when I was in college, in a little apartment in a quaint village outside of Stockholm. Their apartment building was covered in hanging flower baskets and was surrounded by a forest filled with moss-covered trees, soft sunlight, and bright-red toadstools. It was the kind of forest you would read about in a children's book, the type of place you would expect to find a magical creature or two—and the perfect spot for a woodland tea party. I wanted to capture that feeling of enchantment with this whimsical forest gathering.

CREATING THE GATHERING

A woodland tea party is a delightful experience in the great outdoors, but if weather or convenience are a concern, this gathering doesn't have to take place in an enchanted forest. With some attention to detail, a kitchen table can become a perfectly whimsical woodland setting. Natural elements like twigs, moss, and ferns echo details found in the projects in this chapter and turn any room into the perfect setting for a forest tea party when combined with beautiful flowers. Antique tea sets and vintage table linens add a charming, old-fashioned touch and make the table look elegant. You can find beautiful teacups and matching saucers for a deal at local antique stores, secondhand shops, or estate sales.

RECIPES

Ham & Gouda Tea Sandwiches with Sweet Onion Mustard Sauce
Turkey & Lingonberry Tea Sandwiches
Raspberry Cream Cheese Danish Braid (Wienerbrød)
Nutella Swirl Crumb Cake

PROJECTS

Tree Trunk Cake Plate
Teacup Terrariums
Toadstool Garden Picks
Twig Name Tag Flags
Woodland Felt Garland

HAM & GOUDA TEA SANDWICHES WITH
SWEET ONION MUSTARD SAUCE

•))}❂{{(• •))}❂{{(• •))}❂{{(•

These tiny ham and cheese sandwiches are insanely addictive and packed with layer upon layer of Nordic flavor: ham and rye bread are perennial favorites on the Scandinavian lunch table, and Gouda is one of many cheese beloved in the Nordic countries!

MAKES 4 SERVINGS

3 tablespoons
    mayonnaise
2 tablespoons Dijon
    mustard
1 teaspoon finely
    minced shallot
2 shakes Worcestershire
    sauce
½ teaspoon honey
6 slices light rye bread
3 slices black forest ham
3 slices Gouda cheese
1 whole dill pickle

1. In a small bowl, combine the mayonnaise, mustard, shallot, Worcestershire sauce, and honey. Mix with a fork until well combined; set aside.

2. Cut the crusts off the bread, then cut each slice of bread into quarters. Spread the sweet onion mustard sauce on one side of each square of bread. Cut each slice of ham into four long pieces. Fold each piece of ham in half or into thirds (to match the size of the squares of bread), and place a piece of ham on each of the twelve squares of bread. Cut each piece of Gouda into quarters, and place a piece on top of each piece of ham. Cut the pickle into ⅛-inch slices on the diagonal. Place a slice of pickle on top of each piece of cheese. Take the remaining pieces of bread (those with no toppings on them), and place one on top of each slice of pickle, sauce side down.

3. Cover and chill until ready to serve.

> Rose hip tea sounds quite charming, doesn't it? This popular traditional Scandinavian drink is made from the round, ruby-colored part of a rose just below the petals. And since rose hips, or *nyper* in Norwegian, are packed with vitamin C, rose hip tea is good for you too. My grandparents drink a cup every night.

TURKEY & LINGONBERRY TEA SANDWICHES

•⟩⟩⟩✦⟨⟨⟨• •⟩⟩⟩✦⟨⟨⟨• •⟩⟩⟩✦⟨⟨⟨•

Tart red lingonberries are popular in Scandinavian cuisine, and lingonberry preserves are easy to find outside of the region. Most large grocery stores in the United States carry it in the jam and jelly aisle, and if you live near an Ikea store, they always have it on their shelves. The sweet/tart flavor of lingonberries pairs well with the savory turkey and smooth, creamy Havarti cheese in these scrumptious tea sandwiches. If you can't find lingonberry preserves, cranberry sauce will substitute nicely.

MAKES 4 SERVINGS

3 tablespoons
   mayonnaise
1½ tablespoons
   lingonberry preserves
Freshly ground
   black pepper
Pinch of table salt
Squirt of freshly squeezed
   lemon juice
6 slices whole wheat or
   multigrain bread
2 leaves green
   leaf lettuce
4 slices oven-roasted
   turkey breast
4 slices Havarti cheese

1. In a small bowl, combine the mayonnaise, lingonberry preserves, pepper, salt, and lemon juice. Mix with a fork until well combined; set aside.

2. Cut the crusts off the bread, then cut each slice of bread into quarters. Spread the lingonberry mayonnaise on one side of each square of bread. Tear each leaf of lettuce into 2-inch pieces, and place a piece of lettuce on twelve of the squares of bread. Cut each slice of turkey into four long pieces. Fold each piece of turkey in half or into thirds (to match the size of the squares of bread), and place a piece of turkey on top of each piece of bread with lettuce. Cut each piece of Havarti into quarters, and place a piece on top of each piece of turkey. Take the remaining pieces of bread (those with no toppings on them), and place one on top of each slice of cheese, mayonnaise side down.

3. Cover and chill until ready to serve.

RASPBERRY CREAM CHEESE DANISH BRAID
(WIENERBRØD)

⦁>}}>◉{{{⦁ ⦁>}}>◉{{{⦁ ⦁>}}>◉{{{⦁

Breakfast pastries filled with apples or berries or sweetened cheeses, drizzled with frosting or topped with cinnamon and spiced crumbs: we call them Danishes because they come from Denmark. But Scandinavians call them *wienerbrød*, or Viennese bread, because they traditionally have layer after layer of flaky dough in the style of Austrian baked goods. Regardless of what you call them, Danish pastries are delicious. This impressive braided version from my friend Christina uses a sweet roll dough as its base instead of the laminated dough Danish pastries traditionally use, so it's much easier to make and every bit as pretty.

1. Heat the buttermilk gently until it is the temperature of a warm bath. The quickest way to do this is to microwave the milk for 45 to 50 seconds. Add the yeast to the buttermilk along with a pinch of sugar, and let sit 5 minutes, until bubbly (see page xix for tips on making yeast breads).

2. While the yeast is proofing, in a large bowl or in the bowl of a stand mixer fitted with a paddle attachment, beat the butter and sugar on medium speed for about 30 seconds. Add the eggs and beat on medium speed until smooth, about 1 minute. Scrape down the sides of the bowl with a spatula halfway through.

3. In a medium bowl, combine 4 cups of the flour and the salt and baking soda.

4. With the mixer on low speed, gradually add the dry ingredients to the butter-and-sugar mixture, then add the yeast mixture. Beat until smooth.

5. If using a stand mixer, switch to the dough hook attachment. Add the remaining ½ cup flour a little at a time until the dough is no longer sticky when lightly touched, and pulls away from the sides of the bowl.

CONTINUED

MAKES 2 LARGE BRAIDED LOAVES

1 cup plus 2 tablespoons
     buttermilk
1 tablespoon active
     dry yeast
½ cup sugar, plus a pinch
     for proofing the yeast
½ cup butter, softened
2 eggs, at room
     temperature
4½ cups flour, divided
1½ teaspoons table salt
¼ teaspoon baking soda

For the filling:
8 ounces cream cheese,
     softened
1 teaspoon vanilla extract
½ cup confectioners'
     sugar
2 tablespoons butter,
     melted
¾ cup raspberry jam,
     divided

For the icing:
1 cup confectioners' sugar
4 teaspoons whole milk
½ teaspoon vanilla
    extract

Special equipment:
Parchment paper,
    for baking

6. Put the dough in a lightly oiled bowl and cover. Let it rise until doubled in volume, 1 to 1½ hours.

7. While the dough is rising, make the filling. In a medium bowl, beat the cream cheese until smooth. Add the vanilla and confectioners' sugar and beat until smooth. Reserve the melted butter and the jam for step 10.

8. When the dough has doubled in volume, punch it down, turn it out onto a well-floured surface, and knead until it is smooth and soft. Divide the dough into two equal portions. Roll each portion out into a large rectangle, about 12 by 15 inches and ¼ inch thick, and transfer each rectangle to a baking sheet lined with parchment paper.

9. Using a butter knife, lightly divide each rectangle into three equal portions lengthwise. You don't want to cut all the way through the dough; you just want to mark it. Use a pizza wheel to cut the left and right portions of each rectangle into 1-inch horizontal strips. Be sure to cut the same number of strips on both the left and right sides of the dough. Cut the top strips on both the left and right sides off each rectangle, leaving just the 1-inch strip of dough in the center. Repeat on the bottom of each rectangle.

10. Brush the entire surface of both rectangles with the melted butter reserved from step 7. Divide the cream cheese mixture in half, and spread it out along the center portion of each rectangle, staying 1 inch away from the top and bottom. You might have to use your hands to pat the filling out evenly. Spoon half of the jam on top of the cream cheese mixture in each braid and spread it out evenly.

11. Fold the top flap down 1 inch and the bottom flap up 1 inch. Fold the top-left strip of dough over the center. Cross the dough over the center at a slight downward angle so that it just touches the next strip down on the right. Fold the top-right strip down in the same manner. Alternate folding over left and right strips all the way down the pastry. When you get to the last strip of dough on each side, cross it over as usual and tuck any extra dough under the pastry.

12. Cover the dough with plastic wrap and set it in a warm spot to rise for 45 minutes. About 15 minutes before it's done rising, preheat the oven to 350 degrees F.

13. Bake the pastries for 18 to 20 minutes, until puffed and golden. Remove them from the oven and allow to cool.

14. While the Danish braids are cooling, make the icing. In a medium bowl, whisk together the confectioners' sugar, milk, and vanilla until smooth. When braids are cool enough to touch, drizzle with icing. Serve warm or at room temperature.

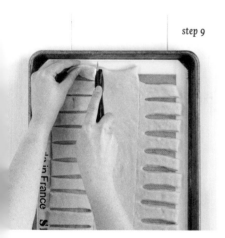
step 9

step 11a

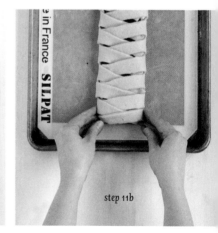
step 11b

NUTELLA SWIRL CRUMB CAKE

❖⟩⟩❖⟨⟨❖ ❖⟩⟩❖⟨⟨❖ ❖⟩⟩❖⟨⟨❖

This cake makes both a sweet end to a tea party and a beautiful centerpiece. Rich chocolate and crunchy hazelnuts are blended into the crumb topping, and a thick swirl of Nutella—a Scandinavian favorite—runs through the middle of the cake. It is as pretty as it is irresistible.

1. Preheat the oven to 350 degrees F. Spray an 8-inch springform pan with nonstick cooking spray and set aside.

2. To make the crumb topping, in a medium bowl, combine the flour, hazelnuts, sugar, and salt. Add the melted butter and stir with a fork until well mixed. Set aside, reserving the chocolate chips for step 7.

3. In the bowl of a stand mixer, combine the butter and sugar. Beat on medium speed until fluffy, about 1 minute. Beat in the egg, then the sour cream and vanilla, until smooth.

4. In a medium bowl, combine the flour, baking powder, baking soda, and salt. Add the dry ingredients to the butter-and-sugar mixture and beat on low speed just until combined. Use a spatula to scrape the sides and bottom of the bowl, then beat on medium speed for 10 seconds to make sure the batter is smooth.

5. Spread the batter evenly in the bottom of the springform pan. The batter will be very thick.

6. Put the Nutella in a heatproof container, and microwave for 30 seconds. Drop small spoonfuls of Nutella on top of the cake batter, scattering them evenly across the surface of the cake. Use a butter knife to swirl the Nutella into the cake batter.

CONTINUED

MAKES 8 SERVINGS

For the crumb topping:
¾ cup flour
½ cup chopped hazelnuts
⅓ cup sugar
Pinch of table salt
¼ cup butter, melted
½ cup semisweet
   chocolate chips

....

¼ cup butter, softened
¾ cup sugar
1 egg
½ cup sour cream
½ teaspoon vanilla
   extract
1 cup flour
½ teaspoon baking
   powder
¼ teaspoon baking soda
¼ teaspoon table salt
½ cup Nutella

Special equipment:
8-inch springform pan

7. Add the reserved chocolate chips from step 2 to the crumb topping. To make sure they are well incorporated, squeeze handfuls of the topping firmly in your hands, then crumble them back into the bowl. Repeat several times until the chocolate chips are coated with crumbs as well.

8. Spread the crumb topping evenly over the top of the cake, then bake it for 48 to 53 minutes, until a toothpick or skewer inserted in the center of the cake comes out clean.

9. Allow the cake to cool in the springform pan for 10 minutes, then remove the sides of the pan and allow the cake to cool completely.

TREE TRUNK CAKE PLATE

⦁⟩⟩⟩❂⟨⟨⟨⦁ ⦁⟩⟩⟩❂⟨⟨⟨⦁ ⦁⟩⟩⟩❂⟨⟨⟨⦁

Since I have such a huge sweet tooth and love to bake, I have somehow amassed an absolutely enormous collection of cake plates. My favorite is this woodsy one I made myself! It's beautiful and natural, and strikes the perfect balance between understated and showstopping.

It's getting easier to find both the large and small wood sections for these cake plates at large arts-and-crafts supply stores. The only trick is finding two pieces that match!

MATERIALS & TOOLS:

Level

1 large slice tree trunk, about 1 inch thick

1 small section log that is wider than it is tall

Sandpaper, belt sander, or sanding table

Pencil

Strong wood glue

Heavy book or can

1. Using a level, make sure the flat surfaces are completely level and smooth on both the tree trunk slice and the log. Use the sandpaper to correct any problems.

2. Decide how you want the two pieces of wood arranged. Choose the most attractive side of the tree trunk slice to be the top of the cake plate. If the log section has a narrower end and a broader end, the narrower end should be at the top, and the broader end should be at the bottom to give the finished cake plate stability.

3. Move the tree trunk slice around on the log section until you find a spot where it balances easily and feels stable. Then, with one hand on the trunk slice and one hand on the log section, flip both pieces upside down without shifting them.

4. With a pencil, lightly trace around the log section where it meets the trunk slice so that you can find this exact placement again.

5. Pick up the log section, apply a generous amount of wood glue to the narrow end, and place it glue side down on top of the tree trunk slice. Make sure to put it in the correct spot. Use the outline you traced to help you place it.

6. Balance a heavy book or can on top of the log to hold it firmly in place while the glue dries.

7. Once the glue is dry, flip the cake stand over and use it! It should be used very gently and wiped clean with a warm, damp cloth as needed.

TEACUP TERRARIUMS

•}}}•❂•{{{• •}}}•❂•{{{• •}}}•❂•{{{•

It's a nice surprise to send guests home from a party with a little gift or memento. These miniature moss-filled terrariums are sure to remind partygoers of their magical afternoon. Matching cups and saucers look sweet, and mismatched pairs have an extra touch of whimsy. Both the teacups and saucers can easily be picked up at an antique shop or secondhand store, and the tiny plants are available in the ground cover section of nurseries and garden centers.

1. Place a shallow layer of the gravel in the bottom of each teacup. It only needs to be about ¼ inch deep.

2. Carefully remove the moss or small plants and their surrounding soil from the containers and place them on top of the gravel in the teacups. Remove any roots or soil that don't fit in the cup. Press the plants down firmly.

3. If necessary, fill in any gaps between the sides of the cups and the soil with extra potting soil, pressing firmly.

4. Water thoroughly and often.

MATERIALS & TOOLS:

Clean small gravel

Teacups with saucers

Moss or small plants

Potting soil

TOADSTOOL GARDEN PICKS

•+}}•❂{{{• •}}}•❂{{{• •}}}•❂{{{•

One of the things I remember most about walking through the forest that surrounded my grandparents' apartment in Sweden was the mushrooms. They had bright-red caps covered in tiny white polka dots and looked like they had been plucked from the pages of a children's book of fairy tales. These handmade garden picks add a rustic woodland touch to the party table and are a sweet gift for guests. They look especially enchanting nestled in the moss of a teacup terrarium.

MATERIALS & TOOLS:

Oven-bake polymer clay in red, yellow, brown, and white

Chopstick or clay-shaping tool

Polymer clay glue

Steel wire

Wire cutters

Ovenproof cup filled with rice

Baking sheet

Oven

1. Open the polymer clay packages. Work with only one color at a time, washing your hands between colors.

2. To make a mushroom cap, take a small chunk of red, yellow, or brown clay and roll it into a ball. Use a flat work surface to flatten one side. You can make oval caps that are flattened on the bottom, wide caps that flare out at the bottom, and caps that turn up at the edges.

3. To make a mushroom stem, take a small chunk of brown or white clay and roll it into a long cylinder, and flatten one end on a work surface. You can make them fat and chunky or long and thin, but if they are too thin they won't maintain their shape.

4. To attach a cap to a stem, use the chopstick or clay-shaping tool to carve out a small hollow on the bottom of the cap that will be just large enough to fit the top of the stem. Put a small amount of polymer clay glue in the hollow and attach the stem to the cap.

5. Gently push the steel wire up through the bottom of the mushroom stem and into the cap a few millimeters. Reshape anything that pops out of place. Use the wire cutters to trim the bottom of the wire, leaving about 2 extra inches sticking out of the bottom of the mushroom.

6. To add dots to a mushroom cap, roll tiny amounts of white polymer clay into balls, flatten them slightly between your thumb and finger, and attach them to the mushroom cap with a small amount of glue.

7. Stick the clay and wire pick into the rice-filled ovenproof cup so that it is standing up, place it on a baking sheet, and bake according to package directions.

8. Allow it to cool completely.

There are lots of different brands of oven-bake polymer clay, and each one has slightly different directions, including oven temperatures and bake times. To avoid problems, make sure all of your clay is the same brand.

TWIG NAME TAG FLAGS

Using homemade place cards at parties can make every guest feel extra special. These whimsical ones are made with twigs and branches, and they help bring the feel of an enchanted forest right to your tea party table.

1. Use the scissors or paper trimmer to cut the red card stock into long rectangles measuring about ¾ by 4 inches (one strip per guest).

2. To make each flag, wrap one strip of the card stock around one end of a thin twig, lining up the edges exactly. Use glue or a piece of double-sided tape to attach the card stock to itself.

3. Cut a triangle out of the free end of the card stock to give it a flag shape.

4. Write each guest's name on a flag using the white gel pen. Allow the marker to dry completely.

5. While the marker is drying, make a hole in the center of each branch slice by using a hammer to pound a nail into the center almost all the way through the branch slice, then pulling it out.

6. Put a small dot of craft glue into each hole, then glue the twig flags into the holes. Allow them to dry.

MATERIALS & TOOLS:

Red card stock

Scissors or paper trimmer

3½-inch-long twigs, 1 per guest

Glue stick or double-sided tape

White fine-tipped gel pen

Thick slices of tree branches, about ¼ inch thick and larger than 1 inch in diameter, 1 per guest

Nail

Hammer

Craft glue

Tree branch slices are available from the wood hobby aisle of the craft store.

If you have a drill with a small-gauge drill bit, it will make holes in your branch slices much faster than a hammer and a nail. Just make sure you use a drill bit that is about the same size around as your twigs.

WOODLAND FELT GARLAND

•⟩⟩⟩◻⟨⟨⟨• •⟩⟩⟩◻⟨⟨⟨• •⟩⟩⟩◻⟨⟨⟨•

Felt has warmth and softness while still being rugged and durable; it's the perfect material for a handmade woodland garland. This example features classic Scandinavian toadstools, earthy leaves, and simple hearts.

MATERIALS & TOOLS:

Photocopier or scanner/printer

Woodland Felt Garland template (page 214)

White card stock

Scissors

Wool blend felt in red, white, tan, and shades of green (see page 208 for exact colors)

Fine-tipped black marker or ink pen

Hot glue gun

Hot glue sticks

Jute twine

White craft paint

Paper plate, cardboard, or something to put the paint on

A paintbrush with a narrow end

1. Photocopy the garland template onto white card stock, and use the scissors to cut out each piece on the solid black line.

2. Lay the pattern pieces on top of the felt. Using the black marker, trace around each piece. Mushroom caps go on red, hearts go on white, stems go on tan, and leaves go on green.

3. Using the scissors, carefully cut out the felt pieces, being sure to stay inside the marker lines.

4. Hot glue the mushroom caps onto mushroom stems. A large *X* on the template shows you where to put the glue on the mushroom stem. Caps should cover the glue completely and overlap stems by about ¼ inch.

5. Lay out the mushrooms, leaves, and hearts and plan their order and spacing.

6. Cut a piece of twine that is your desired length, leaving 12 extra inches on each end for attaching the garland. Lay the twine out on a clean, flat work surface.

7. Put a line of the hot glue across the back of your first felt piece, about ¼ inch down from the top. The dotted lines on the pattern pieces show you where to put the glue. Lay the twine across the felt piece on top of the glue and allow it to cool.

8. Repeat with the remaining felt pieces.

9. Squirt a small amount of the white craft paint onto a small paper plate or piece of cardboard. Spread the paint into a thin layer. Dip the blunt end of the paintbrush into the white paint, and stamp a group of three white dots onto each mushroom cap. Refer to the photo (see below) for placement and spacing.

10. Hang the garland and enjoy!

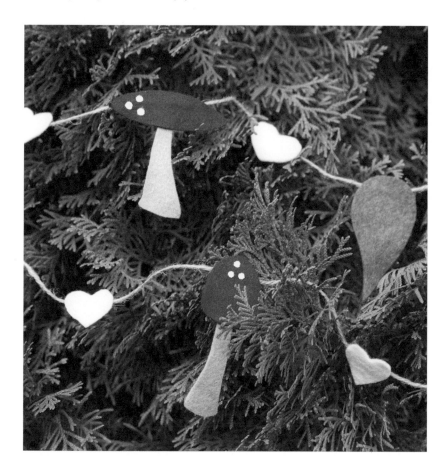

Midsummer Feast

BECAUSE OF THEIR NORTHERN LATITUDES, Scandinavian countries have long, dark winters, which make the light-filled days of summer even more highly prized. In far northern parts of the region, the days are so long at Midsummer that the sun doesn't set at all! Midsummer is one of the biggest annual celebrations in Scandinavian countries, second only to Christmas. Friends and family gather to make crowns from wildflowers, dance around a flower-covered maypole, build glorious bonfires, and eat favorite summer foods. Businesses close their doors, and everyone flocks to the countryside to celebrate the fleeting beauty that is summer in Scandinavia.

CREATING THE GATHERING

Midsummer celebrations are all about being outside and enjoying the beautiful weather. A backyard patio table or card table set up in the garden is a great spot for a Midsummer lunch or dinner. Casual white table linens look crisp and fresh and provide a wonderful backdrop for the abundant floral decorations, fresh greenery, and delicious summer fare. White lights strung in trees or on patio structures lend an air of magic, as do candles tucked in among the flowers on the table, and lawn games like croquet and badminton offer guests good old-fashioned summertime entertainment.

RECIPES

Swedish Meat Pies
Chopped Midsummer Salad with Mangoraja Dressing
Summer Berry Lemonade
Homemade Strawberry Ice Cream

PROJECTS

Fresh Flower Garland
Faux Flower Crowns

SWEDISH MEAT PIES

•))}Ϙ{{(• •))}Ϙ{{(• •))}Ϙ{{(•

Every summer, a little community, called Junction City, near my hometown in western Oregon holds a four-day festival celebrating Scandinavian culture, and it draws crowds from all over the state and beyond. Children perform folk dances dressed in home-made *bunads* (traditional Scandinavian costumes), holding hands and whirling around the stage, stomping their feet and clapping their hands. Members of the festival association, outfitted in impressive Viking garb and horned helmets, wander the crowd and pose for pictures with tourists. There are exhibits and displays featuring Nordic painting, needlework, and crafts. And the food! People line up for blocks to try *aebleskiver* (Danish pancake balls), meatballs and gravy, Finnish funnel cakes, and every kind of Norwegian cookie imaginable. One of the longest food lines every summer is for the Swedish meat pie booth. These tasty pasties are filled with a savory mixture of meat, potatoes, cheese, and spices. My husband has been known to buy them by the dozen and put them in the freezer in case a craving hits. I created my own version of Swedish meat pies so that we can enjoy them fresh all year long.

1. To make the crust, in a large bowl with an electric mixer or in the bowl of a stand mixer fitted with the paddle attachment, beat the butter and sour cream on medium speed until smooth, about 15 seconds. Add the flour and salt, and beat on low just until smooth, about 20 seconds. Wrap the dough in a piece of plastic wrap, and chill it until firm, at least 1 hour.

2. While the dough is chilling, in a large skillet over medium heat, heat the oil. Add the onion, celery, and carrot, and sauté until the onions are translucent, about 10 minutes. Add the garlic and potatoes, and sauté for 2 minutes more, until the garlic is fragrant. Add the ground beef, salt, pepper, nutmeg, and allspice. Crumble the meat, and cook it until the meat is no longer pink, about 5 minutes. Remove the skillet from heat, and stir in the cheddar cheese until evenly distributed. Cover the skillet, and allow the mixture to cool until the crust is thoroughly chilled. Once the beef mixture has cooled slightly, you can put it in the refrigerator to continue cooling while the crust chills.

MAKES 8 PIES

For the crust:
1 cup butter, softened
¾ cup sour cream
2 cups flour
Pinch of table salt

....

2 tablespoons extra-virgin olive oil
1 small onion, finely chopped
2 stalks celery, finely chopped
1 large carrot, peeled and finely chopped
1 clove garlic, minced
2 cups shredded potatoes
1 pound ground beef
½ teaspoon table salt

CONTINUED

Freshly ground black
  pepper
Pinch of ground nutmeg
Pinch of ground allspice
2 cups shredded cheddar
  cheese

3. Preheat the oven to 350 degrees F and line two baking sheets with parchment paper.

4. Divide the chilled dough into eight equal portions. On a well-floured surface, roll each portion of dough into a circle about 8 inches in diameter. Divide the filling into eight equal portions. Place a scoop of filling on one side of a dough circle, and spread the filling out to cover half of the circle. Stay about 1 inch from the edge of the dough, and make sure the filling is only on one side of the circle. Use your finger to lightly brush the edge of the dough circle with water, then fold the dough over the filling and press the edges to seal the pie. Dip a fork in flour, gently press the fork along the edge of the pie to crimp it, then poke two or three holes gently in the top of the pie to let steam escape.

5. Put the pie on a prepared baking sheet, and repeat step 4 to assemble the remaining seven pies.

6. Bake for 30 minutes, or until the crust is golden and bubbly. Allow the pies to cool for at least 5 minutes before serving.

Swedish meat pies actually taste best when they're not piping hot. They get better (and won't burn your mouth) after cooling for a little while. This—plus their portability— makes them great make-ahead party food!

Maypoles are a must at Midsummer celebrations. A giant flower-festooned pole is put up in the middle of a field, and everyone dances around it. Everyone. Young, old, male, female, dressed in traditional costumes or dressed in street clothes—everyone participates in the maypole dances.

CHOPPED MIDSUMMER SALAD WITH MANGORAJA DRESSING

•))⦿(((• •))⦿(((• •))⦿(((•

Skansen is a lovely outdoor folk museum in Stockholm. There are authentic cottages and manor houses, churches, farmsteads, and workshops from over five hundred years of Swedish history, all populated by workers in traditional Scandinavian costumes. My mom and sisters spent a magical Midsummer at Skansen one year. Out of all the fun things they did—making crowns out of fresh flowers and greenery, dancing around a maypole, and eating all of the delicious Swedish food—the thing my mom came home from that vacation raving about was a salad she had at one of the Skansen restaurants. It was full of beautiful colors, flavors, and textures, and it made as big an impression as anything else from the Midsummer festivities. *Mangoraja* is a Swedish condiment that is flavored with curry and mango. It is sweet and creamy, and makes this colorful salad truly unique.

1. In a medium saucepan over high heat, cover the potatoes with cold water, add the salt, and bring the water to a boil. Cook until the potatoes are tender, about 15 minutes. Drain and set aside to cool.

2. While the potatoes are cooking, in a large bowl, combine the tomato, onion, bell peppers, cucumber, beans, and corn. Reserve the bibb lettuce for step 5. When potatoes are cool, add them to the bowl and toss until the ingredients are evenly mixed.

3. To make the vinaigrette, in a blender or in the bowl of a food processor, blend the oil, sugar, vinegar, water, lemon juice, salt, garlic, and pepper until smooth, 20 to 30 seconds. Dress the salad with vinaigrette to taste. Cover and chill until ready to serve.

CONTINUED

MAKES 6 SERVINGS

1 pound small waxy
   potatoes, chopped into
   bite-size pieces
Pinch of table salt
1 large tomato, diced
1 small red onion,
   thinly sliced
1 green bell pepper,
   seeded, deribbed,
   and diced
1 red bell pepper, seeded,
   deribbed, and diced
2 baby cucumbers,
   quartered and sliced
1 (16-ounce) can red
   beans, drained
   and rinsed
1 cup frozen corn, thawed
   and drained
1 small head bibb lettuce,
   cored and torn into
   pieces, for serving

4. To make the *mangoraja* dressing, in the bowl of a food processor, combine the mayonnaise, sour cream, mango chutney, curry, honey, and hot sauce. Pulse until combined but not completely smooth. In a medium bowl, combine the *mangoraja* and salt and pepper to taste.

5. To serve the salad, place a bed of bibb lettuce pieces on a plate. Top with the salad and drizzle with the *mangoraja*.

There are two basic kinds of potatoes: waxy potatoes and starchy potatoes. Waxy potatoes, such as white potatoes, fingerlings, and Yukon Golds, hold their shape well and don't get mushy when cooked.

If you don't have a blender or food processor, you can still make the red wine vinaigrette called for in this recipe. Finely mince the garlic, and, in a container with a tight-fitting lid such as a 16-ounce mason jar, combine all the vinaigrette ingredients. Make sure the lid is securely on the container, then shake vigorously until the dressing is well mixed.

In a pinch, you can use store-bought red wine vinaigrette instead of making your own. Make sure to use a high-quality bottled dressing that has a short list of ingredients and doesn't contain lots of hard-to-pronounce chemicals.

For the vinaigrette:
½ cup extra-virgin olive oil
5 tablespoons sugar
¼ cup red wine vinegar
¼ cup water
1 tablespoon freshly squeezed lemon juice
½ teaspoon table salt
1 clove garlic
Freshly ground black pepper

For the mangoraja dressing:
1 cup mayonnaise
1 cup sour cream
½ cup mango chutney
½ teaspoon curry powder
1 tablespoon honey
Splash of hot sauce
Table salt and freshly ground black pepper

Special equipment:
Blender or food processor

Tradition has it that before going to bed on Midsummer, unmarried women of marriageable age must pick seven different kinds of flowers to put under their pillows. If they do, they are said to dream of their future husband!

SUMMER BERRY LEMONADE

•))⟩❂(((• •))⟩❂(((• •))⟩❂(((•

Summer in Scandinavian countries is berry season, and familiar berries like strawberries, blackberries, blueberries, and raspberries grow alongside berries that are lesser known in the United States, such as cloudberries and lingonberries. This refreshing summer beverage combines the tart flavor of fresh lemons with your favorite juicy berries. Feel free to experiment and find your favorite!

MAKES ABOUT 2 QUARTS

1½ cups fresh lemon
    juice (from 7 to
    8 large lemons)
1¼ cups sugar
8 ounces berries,
    any combination
6 cups cold water

Special equipment:
Blender
Fine mesh sieve
Large pitcher

1. In a blender, combine the lemon juice, sugar, and berries. Blend until smooth, about 30 seconds.

2. Place a fine mesh sieve over the mouth of a pitcher, and pour in the berry puree. Use a big wooden spoon to push as much puree through the strainer as you can. Rinse the spoon off, then use it to scrape off any berry puree that has built up on the underside of the strainer, and add it to the pitcher. Discard the contents of the strainer.

3. Add the water to the pitcher, and use a long-handled spoon to stir. Refrigerate until chilled. Serve over ice.

VARIATIONS:

• Leave out the fruit puree altogether to make a delicious batch of good old-fashioned plain lemonade.

• Use ½ pound peeled, pitted, and coarsely chopped ripe summer peaches in place of the berries to make peach lemonade.

• Elderflower lemonade is uniquely floral and refreshing. To make elderflower lemonade, omit the fruit puree and add elderflower syrup to taste (see page 207 for a list of resources).

HOMEMADE STRAWBERRY ICE CREAM

•))╞◘╡((•))╞◘╡((•))╞◘╡((•

June kicks off strawberry season all across Scandinavia. For as long as anyone can remember, Scandinavian children have spent their summers picking wild, sun-ripened berries and stringing them onto pieces of straw or grass. To me that sounds like the very best use of a summer day. This simple recipe highlights the sweet flavor and rosy color of those most precious summer strawberries.

1. In a blender, combine all of the ingredients, blending until smooth. You will need to work in batches. As you finish each batch, pour it into a large pitcher. When all of the ingredients have been blended and poured into the pitcher, use a long-handled spoon to stir the mixture and make sure it is well combined.

2. Pour the mixture through a fine mesh sieve and into the canister of an ice cream machine. Churn the mixture and freeze it according to the ice cream machine instructions. The ice cream is done churning when it has reached the consistency of soft-serve ice cream.

3. Scoop the ice cream into an airtight container and put it in the freezer to harden.

MAKES ABOUT 3 QUARTS

1 pound fresh or frozen
   strawberries
1 quart half-and-half
2½ cups sugar
½ cup heavy cream
½ cup sour cream
6 tablespoons freshly
   squeezed lemon juice
   (from about
   1½ medium lemons)

Special equipment:
Blender
Large pitcher
Fine mesh sieve
Ice cream machine

This recipe works best in those old-fashioned ice cream machines that have a large-capacity canister and use ice and rock salt to freeze the ice cream. If you only have a smaller ice cream machine (one that makes ice cream using a prefrozen bowl), never fear—you can still make this delicious strawberry treat! You have two options: you can make the full recipe and freeze it in batches, or you can cut the recipe in half.

FRESH FLOWER GARLAND

•›))•❂(((• •›))•❂(((• •›))•❂(((•

Midsummer and fresh flowers were practically made for each other. Floral crowns grace the heads of the womenfolk, and towering maypoles festooned with blossoms preside over community and family gatherings. A garland made of fresh greenery and summer blooms brings the natural beauty of the summer season to the table, and is a fun alternative to the usual dinner party floral centerpiece.

MATERIALS & TOOLS:

12-gauge green floral wire

Wire cutters

Small pruning shears or floral scissors

Flowers and greenery

Green floral tape

24-gauge green floral wire

1. Measure a piece of 12-gauge wire so that it extends the entire length of your table, and trim it with the wire cutters.

2. Use the pruning shears or floral scissors to trim all the flowers and greenery so that they are ready to be arranged. Snip off any dead ends and remove unnecessary leaves. I like to separate mine into piles by variety.

3. Make a small bouquet with some greenery in the back and flowers in the front. Since this is going on a table, it only needs to look great from one side. Use the floral tape to wrap the bouquet tightly about 2 inches from the stem end.

4. Continue making small bouquets until you have used up all of your flowers and greenery. Reserve a few flowers for the final step.

5. Place a bouquet on one end of the 12-gauge wire. Using the thinner 24-gauge wire, securely fasten the bouquet to the thick wire by wrapping it until it feels stable. Trim the wire, and tuck the end behind the bouquet.

6. Place the next bouquet on the thick wire so that it is overlapping with the first bouquet enough to cover any wire and floral tape. Attach the second bouquet with thin wire just like you did in the last step.

7. Continue placing and wrapping bouquets until your thick wire is completely covered. Add the last bouquet going the opposite direction, overlapping the wired section with the previous bouquet's wired section. After placing the garland on the table in its permanent spot, tuck the reserved flowers gently into the garland to cover the wires and fill in the space between the last two bouquets.

This fresh flower garland will only look its best for a few hours after being made. Be sure to make it the same day you want to use it, and store it in a cool place until needed.

What day is Midsummer? Well, it depends on who you ask! Technically, Midsummer is the summer solstice, the longest day of the year, which usually falls around June 21. But over the years, each country in Scandinavia has adapted its Midsummer celebration to suit its needs. In Norway and Denmark Midsummer is always celebrated on June 23, while in Finland and Sweden it is always on a Saturday between June 20 and 26.

FAUX FLOWER CROWNS

Midsummer crowns are made of beautiful, fresh greenery and wildflowers. They adorn the head of every fair maiden in attendance at any Midsummer celebration. They are lush and gorgeous . . . and fleeting. The only bad thing about fresh flower crowns is their incredibly short lifespan—you only get to wear them once! Flower crowns made with faux flowers and greenery are equally beautiful and have the added bonus of lasting forever, so you can wear them even after your Midsummer feast.

1. Wrap the length of greenery garland around your head (or the head of the person for whom you are making the crown) until the edges touch. Add another 2 inches past the place where the ends overlap, and use the wire cutters to cut the garland. Wrap the overlapped ends of the garland tightly with green floral tape until the crown is secure.

2. Trim the silk flowers so that their stems are about 3 inches long, and trim off any greenery along the stems. Gather small bunches of three or four flowers into little bouquets, and tightly wrap the stems with the floral tape.

3. Tuck these small bouquets into the greenery garland crown, and secure them with more floral tape. Add bouquets all around the crown, or put a big cluster on one side to be worn over the ear.

MATERIALS & TOOLS:

Silk greenery garland

Wire cutters

Green floral tape

Small silk flowers

Lots of faux greenery comes in plastic now, which looks very realistic but gets tangled easily in hair. Try to find softer materials for your garland, such as fabric or silk.

Afternoon Fika

FIKA IS A TRADITIONAL DAILY Swedish coffee break where friends, family, or coworkers gather to enjoy their coffee with a bite to eat—open-faced sandwiches, breads, cakes, and pastries—in the middle of the afternoon. It's kind of like the Scandinavian equivalent of Italy's *riposo* or Spain's siesta: it's a time to step away from work or school or busyness for a moment and just relax.

CREATING THE GATHERING

Fika is casual by nature, so there's no need to get fancy. Set out stacks of plates and coffee mugs, plenty of paper napkins, lots of freshly baked treats, and, of course, coffee! I think every gathering is better with fresh flowers, but you don't have to break the bank on fancy bouquets for your coffee break. Most grocery stores carry nice bouquets of fresh flowers that are fairly inexpensive, and with a little trimming and rearranging, they look beautiful. And be sure to provide places to sit and chat. Relaxing and making connections is what *fika* is all about!

RECIPES

Braided Cardamom Bread (Finnish Pulla)
Open-Faced Sandwiches with Herbed Cream Cheese & Baby Cucumbers
Spiced Apple Coffee Cake

PROJECTS

No-Sew Inlaid Felt Coasters
Hand-Printed Fika Mugs
Floral Folk-Art Serving Tray

BRAIDED CARDAMOM BREAD (FINNISH PULLA)

•}}}❂{{{• •}}}❂{{{• •}}}❂{{{•

I first heard about braided cardamom bread, or Finnish *pulla*, from my friend Tania, who doesn't have a Scandinavian bone in her body, but who knows a delicious recipe when she sees one! Her family has been making this bread for years and years, and it is as versatile as it is delicious. It makes a fantastic base for cinnamon rolls, but it is also wonderful topped with just a sprinkle of Swedish pearl sugar. It tastes best when eaten within two days of baking (usually sliced thick and slathered with butter), but the leftovers make insanely good French toast.

MAKES 2 LARGE BRAIDED LOAVES

2 cups whole milk

⅔ cup sugar

½ cup butter

2 packets active dry yeast or instant yeast

6 cups flour, divided

¾ teaspoon table salt

2 teaspoons ground cardamom

2 eggs, divided

1 tablespoon whole milk

2 tablespoons Swedish pearl sugar (see page 207 for more on pearl sugar)

1. In a small saucepan, combine the milk and sugar; whisk until the sugar is dissolved. Add the butter, and heat over medium low, stirring gently, until the butter is melted. Remove from the heat.

2. Allow the milk mixture to cool to the temperature of a warm bath (not hot!), and stir in the yeast. Allow the mixture to sit for 5 minutes to make sure the yeast is active and alive. You should see bubbles on the surface, and the mixture should grow in volume (see page xix for tips on making yeast breads).

3. When you are certain the yeast is working, in a large bowl with a wooden spoon or in the bowl of a stand mixer fitted with the dough hook attachment, add the milk mixture. Add 2 cups of the flour, and the salt, cardamom, and 1 of the egg. Mix until combined.

4. Add 3 more cups of the flour and stir until it is completely incorporated. Add the remaining 1 cup flour a little at a time until the dough forms a ball and is no longer sticky when lightly touched with your finger. You might not use the entire cup of flour.

5. Transfer the dough to a large, lightly oiled bowl, cover it with plastic wrap, and let it rise in a warm spot until doubled in size, about 1 hour.

CONTINUED

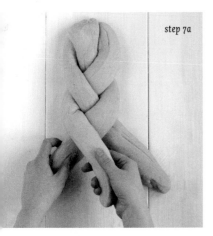

step 7a

step 7b

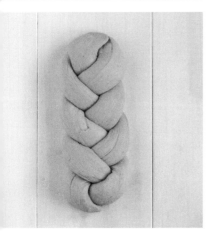

6. Punch down the dough, knead by hand for 1 to 2 minutes on a well-floured surface, and let it rest for 10 minutes.

7. Divide the dough into six equal portions. Roll each portion into a skinny rope about 15 inches long. Line up three dough ropes side by side on the counter in front of you. Pinch one end of each rope together, then gently braid the three ropes into a loaf. When you reach the end, pinch the remaining dough together and tuck it under the loaf slightly. Repeat with the other three dough ropes to make a second loaf.

8. Place each loaf on a parchment-lined baking sheet, and let it rise for 30 minutes.

9. Preheat the oven to 375 degrees F.

10. To make an egg wash, in a small bowl, whisk the remaining 1 egg and the milk together. Brush the top and sides of both braided loaves with the egg wash, then sprinkle each loaf with 1 tablespoon pearl sugar.

11. Bake the loaves until browned on top, about 20 minutes. Remove from the oven and allow them to cool before slicing.

Swedish pearl sugar is made of little pellets of sugar that have been pressed together, like sugar cubes, only much smaller. It is available online through Amazon and King Arthur Flour. You can also find it in person at any Ikea store and many well-stocked grocery stores.

If you absolutely cannot find Swedish pearl sugar anywhere, put a few sugar cubes in a small ziplock bag, seal the bag, and crush the cubes lightly with a hammer, a mallet, or the back of a big spoon. You don't want to completely pulverize them; you just want to make smaller chunks, about the size of a grain of rice.

OPEN-FACED SANDWICHES WITH HERBED CREAM CHEESE & BABY CUCUMBERS

•))┼❂┼((• •))┼❂┼((• •))┼❂┼((•

When I was growing up, whenever my siblings and I had a family heritage or countries of the world project to do at school, we always chose Norway as our topic. And we always made sure to mention open-faced sandwiches. They made a big impression on our young minds. Open-faced sandwiches are a part of daily life all across Scandinavia. You can eat them for breakfast, lunch, or an afternoon snack. You can use sliced bread or crisp crackers, and any number of toppings, from butter and cheese to radishes and hard-boiled eggs. This version features a homemade cream cheese spread filled with fresh herbs.

1. In a medium bowl, combine the cream cheese, scallion, parsley, chives, dill, garlic, lemon juice, salt, and pepper. Reserve a small amount of fresh dill for garnish. Mix until everything is evenly distributed. Cover and chill the mixture at least 1 hour before serving.

2. Spread 1 to 2 tablespoons of the cream cheese mixture on a crispbread cracker. Repeat until all of the cream cheese mixture has been used. Top with the baby cucumber slices, and sprinkle with the reserved fresh dill. Eat immediately.

VARIATIONS:

• Instead of the baby cucumbers, top the herbed cream cheese mixture with smoked salmon and very thinly sliced red onions.

• For a heartier snack, use thin slices of European rye bread instead of the crispbread crackers. It can be found in the bread aisle of higher-end grocery stores, and is usually packaged in little bricks. It tastes best lightly toasted.

MAKES 4 SERVINGS

8 ounces cream cheese, softened
1 scallion, finely minced
1 tablespoon finely chopped fresh parsley
1 tablespoon snipped fresh chives
1 tablespoon finely snipped fresh dill, plus more for garnish
1 clove garlic, finely minced
1 teaspoon freshly squeezed lemon juice
Pinch of table salt
Freshly ground black pepper
Crispbread crackers, for serving
Baby cucumbers, for serving

CONTINUED

Crispbread crackers look kind of like our American graham crackers: they are large, brownish rectangles dotted with tiny indentations. Unlike graham crackers, they are savory instead of sweet. They are always made with rye but come in a variety of delicious flavors. Some common brands are RyKrisp and Wasa. You can find them in the cracker aisle at your grocery store.

Smørrebrød is a Danish word meaning *butter and bread*, and it is a staple of Danish cuisine. Danes love their open-faced sandwiches, and besides butter, they top their bread with sliced cucumbers or radishes, smoked fish, herbs, pickled vegetables, hard-boiled eggs, meats, spreads, relishes, and more.

Rugbrød is a Danish rye bread that serves as the base for Denmark's famous open-faced sandwiches. It usually contains sourdough starter and lots of rye flour, and it can be plain or packed with a variety of seeds. There are a few Danish bakeries scattered throughout the United States that make it fresh, so if you're lucky enough to find one, make sure to try a slice! (See page 207 for more on rye bread.)

SPICED APPLE COFFEE CAKE

•))) ❂ (((• •))) ❂ (((• •))) ❂ (((•

This recipe is really two delicious cakes rolled into one. It combines a Scandinavian favorite, apple cake, with a fika must-have, coffee cake, and the result is twice as nice. Warm spices, bits of tart apple, and a sweet, sugary crumb topping make it an irresistible coffee table addition. You'll find yourself wanting to sneak a piece for dessert and another for breakfast!

MAKES 12 TO 16 SERVINGS

For the crumb topping:
1¼ cups flour
⅓ cup granulated sugar
⅓ cup lightly packed light brown sugar
½ teaspoon ground cinnamon
¼ teaspoon table salt
½ cup butter, melted

. . . .

½ cup butter, softened
1½ cups sugar
2 eggs
1 cup sour cream
1 teaspoon vanilla extract
2 cups flour
1 teaspoon baking powder
1 teaspoon ground cinnamon
1 teaspoon ground cardamom
½ teaspoon baking soda
½ teaspoon ground nutmeg
½ teaspoon table salt
2 medium apples, peeled, cored, and diced

For the icing:
1 cup confectioners' sugar
1 to 2 tablespoons whole milk, plus more as needed

1. To make the crumb topping, in a medium bowl, combine the flour, sugars, cinnamon, and salt. Add the butter and mix with a fork until combined; set aside.

2. Preheat the oven to 350 degrees F, and grease a 9-by-13-inch baking pan.

3. In a large bowl with an electric mixer or in the bowl of a stand mixer fitted with the paddle attachment, beat the butter and sugar on medium speed until fluffy, about 1 minute. Add the eggs one at a time, beating for 10 seconds after each addition. Add the sour cream and vanilla, and beat until combined.

4. In a medium bowl, combine the flour, baking powder, cinnamon, cardamom, baking soda, nutmeg, and salt. Add the dry ingredients to the mixer, and beat on low speed until combined. Scrape down the sides of the bowl and beat again briefly.

5. Fold in the apples.

6. Spread the batter evenly in the baking pan, and top with the reserved crumb topping. Bake for 40 to 43 minutes, until a skewer inserted in the center of the cake comes out clean. Allow it to cool.

7. While the cake is cooling, make the icing. In a small bowl, combine the confectioners' sugar and milk, whisking until smooth. Add more milk, whisking constantly, until it reaches a thick, syrupy consistency. When the cake is warm but not hot, drizzle the icing over the top. Allow the cake to cool completely before cutting and serving.

NO-SEW INLAID FELT COASTERS

∘⟩⟩⟩✪⟨⟨⟨∘ ∘⟩⟩⟩✪⟨⟨⟨∘ ∘⟩⟩⟩✪⟨⟨⟨∘

Some people are dyed-in-the-wool coaster users and some aren't. But whether or not you have a deep-seated need to protect your tabletop, these brightly colored felt coasters add a cheery pop of color to your coffee table. And they are a quick and easy project, no sewing machine required!

MATERIALS & TOOLS:

No-Sew Inlaid Felt Coasters template (page 212)

Plain white paper

Pen

Scissors

Wool-blend felt in red and white (see page 208 for exact colors)

Ruler or measuring tape

Single-hole paper punch

Scrap cardboard, about the size of a cereal box

Spray adhesive

Craft glue

Pinking shears

1. Turn to the coaster template. Lay the paper over it, and trace the circle with a pen, then use the scissors to cut the circle out.

2. Trace three circles on the red felt and then cut them out.

3. Use the ruler and pen to mark sixteen dots evenly spaced around one red felt circle, about ½ inch from the edge. It works best to make the first dot, then make the next directly across the circle from it. Make two more dots halfway between the two previous dots, one on either side of the circle. Keep making dots halfway between the existing dots until you have sixteen dots drawn. Use the hole punch to punch out each dot. Stay ½ inch away from the edge. Punching holes in felt takes some care. Make sure you clean each punched felt circle out of the hole punch before making the next hole.

4. Punch sixteen holes out of white felt and reserve the punched pieces.

5. Lay out the cardboard on the grass or sidewalk outside. Lay one red felt circle without holes in it on top, and spray it evenly with spray adhesive. Quickly but carefully lay the other red felt circle without holes in it on top of it, making sure the circles are aligned. Spray the second red felt circle evenly with spray adhesive, and place the punched red felt circle on top of it, again working quickly but carefully, and lining up the edges of the circles.

6. Put a very small dab of craft glue inside each punched hole. Put a white felt dot in each hole. Press the dots in firmly so that the surface of the felt is mostly even. Allow all of the glue to dry completely.

7. Use the pinking shears to trim the edge of the coaster into a zigzag. Place the pinking shears just inside the edge of the circle so that the outer part of each zigzag lines up with the outside of the circle. As you work your way around the circle and approach your starting point, cut very slowly and try to line up the last point right next to the first point.

Have you heard of egg coffee? It's an old-fashioned method of brewing coffee that is popular in Sweden and Norway and in the Midwest where there are lots of Americans with Scandinavian ancestry. You mix coffee grounds with an egg (you can even use the shell!), heat it, and strain it. It makes a really clear, flavorful brew without any bitterness!

step 1

step 2a

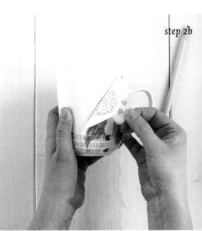

step 2b

HAND-PRINTED FIKA MUGS

•)}}❂{{(• •)}}❂{{(• •)}}❂{{(•

These hand-printed mugs feature the word *fika* decorated with folk art–inspired flowers. They might seem tricky to make, but thanks to a simple tracing technique, they are practically foolproof. Each *fika* mug looks cute on its own, and together, they make a fun, colorful set.

1. Use a pencil to trace the backward designs from the mug template onto a sheet of paper. Trace one set of designs for each mug you want to make, leaving several inches of blank space between sets. Use the scissors to cut out each set. There's no need to be detailed; just cut a rectangle around each word and flower combination. You can use the same design on each mug, or mix and match the flowers and text to create a whole set of unique dishes.

2. Tape one design set onto a mug so that the design is positioned where you want it, with the pencil-covered side touching the mug. Pressing firmly, color over the paper with a pencil. There's no need to be neat here; just scribble over it. This will lightly transfer the design onto the mug. Remove the paper and discard it. Repeat with the remaining designs and mugs.

3. Using the paint pen, carefully trace over the designs on the mugs. Be sure to go from left to right on each mug so that you don't smear wet paint. Let the finished mugs dry for 24 hours.

4. Put the dry mugs in the oven, then preheat the oven to 300 degrees F. Once the oven is up to temperature, bake the mugs for 35 minutes. Turn off the oven and allow the mugs to cool in the oven as the oven cools. It is imperative that you put the mugs in the oven before turning it on, and that you leave them in the oven until it has cooled off completely. Putting the mugs in a hot oven or pulling them out before they have cooled could result in broken mugs. Let the mugs cool completely before using.

5. After baking, your Fika mugs should be dishwasher safe, but gentle handwashing is always a good alternative.

MATERIALS & TOOLS:

Pencil

Hand-Printed Fika Mugs template (page 216)

Plain white paper

Scissors

Masking tape or painter's tape

Plain white porcelain mugs

Fine-tipped Pebeo Porcelaine 150 China paint pen in Anthracite black

FLORAL FOLK-ART SERVING TRAY

⊹}}}⊙{{{⊹ ⊹}}}⊙{{{⊹ ⊹}}}⊙{{{⊹

You've probably seen *rosemåling* before, even if the word is new to you. It's a style of Norwegian folk painting that features leaves, flowers, geometric patterns, and lush scroll-work. Since my family is very proud of its Norwegian heritage, and since both my mom and nana were really interested in folk painting when I was growing up, I've been sur-rounded by *rosemåling* for as long as I can remember. Hand-painted *velkommen* signs, Scandinavian holiday décor, decorative plates, and wall hangings have always graced the homes of my parents and grandparents. The colors and floral design of this sweet serving tray were inspired by the *rosemåling* I grew up with.

MATERIALS & TOOLS:

Plain wooden serving tray

Sandpaper

Garbage bags
or newspaper

Light-blue satin or matte
finish spray paint (see
page 208 for exact color)

Pencil

Floral Folk-Art Serving
Tray template
(page 218)

Plain white paper

Masking tape

Craft paint (see page 219
for a color guide and page
208 for exact colors used)

Soft-bristled paint
brushes

Clear acrylic sealer spray

1. Lightly sand the edges and surfaces of a wooden serving tray so that they are smooth.

2. Working outside or in a well-ventilated area, put garbage bags or newspaper on the ground to protect it from paint. A protected area about 4 by 4 feet should be big enough. Put the wooden serving tray on the center of the garbage bags, and spray the tray with the light-blue paint following the application directions on the spray-paint can. Add as many coats as necessary (one to two), and allow the tray to dry completely.

3. Use a pencil to trace the design from the serving tray template onto a sheet of plain white paper. Center the design on the tray, pencil side down, and tape it in place.

4. Pressing firmly, color over the paper with a pencil. There's no need to be neat here; just scribble all over it. This will transfer the design onto the tray. Remove the paper and discard it.

5. Use the paint brushes to fill in the design outline. Use the color guide on page 219 to see what color to make each section. Allow one color of paint to dry completely before moving on to the next color.

6. After the tray is dry, spray the entire thing with the acrylic sealer to seal it. Don't skip this step! Acrylic sealer will make the tray more durable.

Even though the tray is sealed after being painted, it still needs to be protected and handled with care. Don't put anything hot on the tray, and don't put food directly on it. Under absolutely no circumstances should you put it in the dishwasher. To clean it, wipe it with a slightly damp cloth and allow it to air-dry.

step 3

step 4

Summer Seafood Celebration

SCANDINAVIANS ARE MASTER FISHERMEN and equally masterful at feasting on the ocean's bounty. Seafood is a major component of their diet year-round: oysters, mussels, lobster, salmon, cod, mackerel, king crab, herring, shrimp, and more are available at various times of the year. But summer, with its warm weather and lingering daylight, is the perfect time of year to gather for a seafood feast.

CREATING THE GATHERING

If at all possible, this celebration should take place outdoors on a warm summer evening. For a fancy gathering, use a crisp white tablecloth. For a more casual dinner, cover the table with rolls of white butcher paper. Wicker or straw chargers under white dinner plates give the table a beachy look that pairs well with the nautical knots tied around the napkins. Low, wide floral centerpieces look lovely on the table and don't get in the way of friendly conversation. White flowers are a nice touch on top of the white table linens. Homemade citronella candles will add a soft glow and refreshing fragrance, and will help keep pesky summer bugs away from your guests.

RECIPES

Poached Salmon with Dill Sauce
Seafood Salad with Summer Herbs
Dill Muffin Dinner Rolls
Blueberry Custard Pie (Finnish Mustikkapiirakka)

PROJECTS

Mason Jar Citronella Candles
Hanging Paper Fan Decorations
Nautical Rope Napkin Knots

POACHED SALMON WITH DILL SAUCE

•}}}❂{{{• •}}}❂{{{• •}}}❂{{{•

My nana and poppy got this recipe from a friend while living in Sweden, and they say it is the most delicious way to cook salmon. And it couldn't be easier! No one wants to spend their summer evening slaving away in a hot kitchen. This tasty seafood dish, including the vibrant dill sauce, is ready in a heartbeat.

MAKES 4 SERVINGS

1 tablespoon white
   vinegar
Table salt
4 (6-ounce) fillets salmon

For the sauce:
1 cup packed fresh dill
1 small green onion
½ cup mayonnaise
½ cup sour cream
1 tablespoon white
   vinegar

Special equipment:
Blender or food processor

1. To poach the salmon, in a wide, deep skillet with a lid, add 1 inch of water. Add the vinegar, and bring the liquid to a boil over medium heat.

2. Lightly salt the salmon, and add it, skin side down, to the poaching liquid.

3. Cover, reduce the heat until the liquid barely simmers, and cook for 5 to 10 minutes, until the fish is cooked through. The cooking time will depend on the thickness of the salmon fillets.

4. While the salmon is cooking, make the dill sauce. In a blender or in the bowl of a food processor, combine the dill, green onion, mayonnaise, sour cream, and vinegar. Process until smooth.

5. Using a slotted spoon, remove the cooked salmon from the skillet. Serve topped with the dill sauce.

> August is crayfish season in Sweden. Restaurants and homes host crayfish parties, or *kräftskiva*, as they are called in Sweden. They decorate with brightly colored Chinese lanterns that look like the man in the moon, and serve piles of the bright-red crustaceans that have been boiled with fresh dill.

SEAFOOD SALAD WITH SUMMER HERBS

❖•))}❖{{{•❖ •))}❖{{{•❖ •))}❖{{{•❖

During the summer months, seafood salad is served all across Scandinavia as a side dish, main dish, smorgasbord staple, and open-faced sandwich topping. This recipe comes from Peter Sproul, director of culinary arts at the Culinary Arts Institute at Utah Valley University. Peter's niece, Eva Jorgensen of Sycamore Street Press, has been my good friend since college. Her family enjoys this seafood salad often at family gatherings, where she says it is always a hit!

1. Cut the crab meat and shrimp into 1-inch pieces. (If you get very small shrimp and flaked crab meat, you can skip this step.)

2. In a large bowl, combine the crab meat, shrimp, celery, and green onions. Finely chop the herbs, add them to the bowl, and set aside.

3. In a medium bowl, whisk together the lemon juice and zest, mayonnaise, sour cream, Old Bay Seasoning, salt, and pepper.

4. Add the mayonnaise mixture to the crab mixture, stir well to combine, cover, and chill for 4 hours to let the flavors blend. Serve on a bed of lettuce leaves or on top of sliced bread.

MAKES 8 TO 10 SERVINGS

1½ pounds cooked crab meat
1 pound cooked shrimp
3 cups finely chopped celery (from about 8 stalks celery)
2 bunches of green onions, finely chopped (white and light-green parts only)
1 cup loosely packed fresh herbs such as dill, chervil, thyme, basil, oregano, flat-leaf parsley, and tarragon
1 small lemon, juiced and zested
1½ cups mayonnaise
⅔ cup sour cream or crème fraîche
3 teaspoons Old Bay Seasoning
1 teaspoon table salt
Freshly ground black pepper
Lettuce leaves or sliced bread, for serving (optional)

Where does all of the fresh seafood in Scandinavia come from? Almost everywhere you look in Scandinavia, there's a body of water. West of Norway is the Norwegian Sea, which runs into the North Sea as it, ironically, heads south. There's also the Gulf of Bothnia, which sits between Sweden and Finland, and the Baltic Sea, which is farther south, between Sweden and Estonia. And there are over 855,000 lakes spread out across Norway, Sweden, Denmark, and Finland. Lots of water equals lots of seafood!

DILL MUFFIN DINNER ROLLS

∙⟩⟩⟩❁⟨⟨⟨∙ ∙⟩⟩⟩❁⟨⟨⟨∙ ∙⟩⟩⟩❁⟨⟨⟨∙

I remember having dill muffins as a child and not liking them. As an adult who now thinks they're delicious, I'm not exactly sure what got into me back then! These muffin-shaped dinner rolls have everything I love best in baked goods: they are buttery and savory and slightly salty, with a toasty dill flavor from the dill seed. They go great with the seafood recipes in this chapter, but are also fantastic all-purpose dinner rolls.

MAKES 12 MUFFINS

1 packet active dry yeast
¼ cup warm water
2 tablespoons sugar, plus
    a pinch for proofing
    the yeast
1 cup cottage cheese
1 egg
1 tablespoon dried
    minced onion
1 tablespoon butter,
    melted
2 teaspoons dried
    dill seed
1 teaspoon table salt
¼ teaspoon baking soda
2¼ to 2½ cups flour
Butter, for garnish
Chopped fresh baby dill,
    for garnish

1. In a glass measuring cup, combine the yeast and warm water with a pinch of sugar. Let sit in a warm spot for 5 minutes, or until the mixture is bubbly and has increased in volume (see page xix for tips on making yeast breads).

2. In a large bowl with a wooden spoon or in the bowl of a stand mixer fitted with the dough hook attachment, combine the cottage cheese, egg, sugar, onion, melted butter, dill seed, salt, and baking soda. Add the yeast mixture and mix until combined.

3. Add 2 cups of the flour and mix until smooth. Continue adding flour in ¼-cup increments until the dough is smooth and no longer sticky when lightly touched. You might not use all of the flour.

4. Put the dough in a lightly oiled bowl, cover with plastic wrap, and let it rise until doubled in volume, 50 minutes to 1 hour.

5. Preheat the oven to 350 degrees F and lightly spray a 12-cup muffin tin with nonstick cooking spray.

6. Punch down the risen dough and knead it for 1 to 2 minutes on a lightly floured surface. Divide the dough into twelve equal portions. Place a portion of dough in each cup.

7. Cover the muffin tins with plastic wrap and allow the muffins to rise for 20 more minutes.

8. Bake the muffins for 20 to 25 minutes, or until puffed and golden. Remove from the oven, rub the tops with the butter, and sprinkle with baby dill.

BLUEBERRY CUSTARD PIE
(FINNISH MUSTIKKAPIIRAKKA)

•}}}❂{{{• •}}}❂{{{• •}}}❂{{{•

My friend Marcelle spent some time living in Finland in her twenties and is my expert on all things Finnish. When I asked her about this recipe, she told me that *piirakka* means pie, but that Finns use the word *pie* just as generously as we do in America. It can mean actual pie, or hand pies, or even fruit-filled cookie bars. *Piirakka* can be sweet or savory, filled with fruit or meat or eggs or rice. This version, featuring ripe blueberries surrounded by a tangy custard filling, is the very quintessence of a summer dessert—fresh, fruity, and delicious.

MAKES 8 SERVINGS

1¼ cups flour
¼ cup sugar
¼ teaspoon table salt
½ cup cold butter,
   cut into pieces
1 egg yolk
1 tablespoon cold water
1 teaspoon vanilla extract

For the filling:
2 eggs
⅔ cup plain yogurt
   (low-fat or whole
   milk yogurt)
½ cup heavy cream
⅓ cup sugar
1 teaspoon freshly
   squeezed lemon juice
1 teaspoon vanilla extract
½ teaspoon cornstarch
Pinch of table salt
2 cups fresh or frozen
   blueberries
Lightly sweetened
   whipped cream, for
   serving (optional)

1. Preheat the oven to 325 degrees F.

2. To make the dough for the crust, in the bowl of a food processor, pulse the flour, sugar, and salt briefly to combine. Add the butter, and pulse about ten times. Add the egg yolk, water, and vanilla, and process just until the dough starts to form clumps. Press the dough into the bottom and up the sides of a 9-inch pie pan, and chill while making the filling.

3. To make the filling, in a blender, combine the eggs, yogurt, cream, sugar, lemon juice, vanilla, cornstarch, and salt. Blend until smooth, 20 to 30 seconds.

4. Spread the blueberries evenly in the chilled crust and put it on a baking sheet. Pour the filling over the blueberries in the pan, slide the baking sheet and pie pan into the oven, and bake for 60 to 65 minutes, or until the pie is deeply golden and a knife inserted in the center comes out mostly clean. If the edges of the piecrust begin to look brown before the filling is finished baking, lay a few strips of aluminum foil just across the outside edge of the pie to prevent the crust from browning further.

5. Allow the pie to cool completely before serving. Serve topped with the whipped cream.

VARIATIONS:

• In Finland, jam made with a mix of blueberries and raspberries is called *queen jam*. To make a queen custard pie, simply use 1 cup fresh blueberries and 1 cup fresh raspberries.

• You can make this custard pie with any kind of berry you fancy or with a mix of your favorite fresh berries. Just remember to use 2 cups of berries total.

Special equipment:
Food processor
Blender
9-inch pie pan

MASON JAR CITRONELLA CANDLES

•)))⬥(((• •)))⬥(((• •)))⬥(((•

There are many wonderful things about summer: the long evenings that stretch out for hours; the warm, balmy weather; the fresh, mouthwatering foods. But one of the things that's not so great about warmer weather and lingering twilight is the bugs. Nothing spoils an outdoor party like an infestation of pesky flies or buzzing mosquitoes. These citronella candles in decorative mason jars add a charming touch to your gathering while helping keep the bugs at bay.

MATERIALS & TOOLS:

12 (8-ounce) or
24 (4-ounce) clean
widemouthed mason jars

Baking sheet lined with
aluminum foil

Wick adhesive or
double-sided tape

Tabbed wicks

Pencil with eraser

Masking tape

Medium pot dedicated to
crafting, or a large, clean
coffee can

4 pounds soy wax chips

1 fluid ounce citronella
essential oil (not tiki torch oil)

1 fluid ounce lavender
essential oil

Bamboo skewer or long-
handled wooden spoon
dedicated to crafting

Oven mitts

1. Place all of the mason jars on the aluminum foil–lined baking sheet. Put your adhesive of choice on the bottom of each wick tab, and carefully stick a wick into the bottom of each jar. Make sure the wicks are centered in their jars, and press firmly with the eraser end of the pencil to secure.

2. Stretch two pieces of masking tape across the center of each jar, one on each side of the wick, to hold each wick in place.

3. In a medium pot over medium-low heat, melt the soy wax chips until completely melted and clear. Add the essential oils to the wax and stir with a bamboo skewer for 1 minute more to distribute the oils.

4. With oven mitts on, pour the hot wax carefully into the prepared jars and allow them to cool overnight.

5. When the jars are cool, remove the masking tape. Cut enough rope to wrap around the top of each jar just under the rim. Put a thin line of hot glue around the jar, place the rope over it, and hold it in place until the glue dries.

6. Trim the wicks to ¼ inch before burning.

CONTINUED

12 inches (¼-inch) manila
rope per candle

Heavy-duty scissors

Hot glue gun

Hot glue sticks

Once you have used a pot or spoon for making candles, you really shouldn't use it for making food ever again! So use an old pot and spoon that don't see much action, or buy a pot specifically for making candles and doing crafts. You can find old pots at thrift stores or garage sales, and most large craft stores sell inexpensive pots in the same aisle as their other candle-making supplies.

After filling your jars with melted wax, be sure to clean out your pot thoroughly with paper towels while the wax is still liquid. Just wipe out as much as you possibly can.

step 2

HANGING PAPER FAN DECORATIONS

•⟩⟩✦❁✦⟨⟨• •⟩⟩✦❁✦⟨⟨• •⟩⟩✦❁✦⟨⟨•

These pleated paper fans are a nod to the brightly colored Chinese fans and lanterns that are hung at seafood feasts during summers in Scandinavia. The store-bought fans are usually bright yellow, red, and blue, with happy faces printed on them. These home-made ones, with their ocean-inspired color palette, are a simpler, more elegant version. Make several in different shades of blue paper, and hang them from a patio or umbrella for a pop of color.

1. Accordion-fold each sheet of paper. Use the ruler to make sure each fold is 1 inch wide. It doesn't matter if you fold widthwise or lengthwise, as long as you fold each piece of paper the same way. You can use a bone folder to make your creases nice and sharp. If you don't have a bone folder, the edge of a ruler will work just as well.

2. When all sheets of paper are pleated, use the glue or double-sided tape to tape them together one after the other. Depending on how you folded your paper, you might have to tape two front sides together or tape one piece of paper slightly overlapping the next.

3. Use the scissors to cut a 36-inch length of twine or string. While holding the bunch of pleated paper together, tie the string around the middle of the paper. Use the ruler to make sure you have the string centered. Tie a nice, tight knot, and *do not* trim the strings.

4. Pull the top-left and bottom-left edges of the paper fans down so that they meet in the middle, and tape or glue the two edges together. Repeat for the top-right and bottom-right edges as well. Before you tape the last two sections of pleated paper together, sandwich the strings or twine pieces between them so that they run from the center out to the edge. Tape the two paper sections together with the strings between them.

5. Use the strings to hang your fan.

MATERIALS & TOOLS:

3 pieces of matching patterned or solid blue paper (not card stock), either 8½ by 11 or 12 by 12 inches

Ruler

Bone folder (optional)

Glue stick or double-sided tape

Scissors

Baker's twine or string

CONTINUED

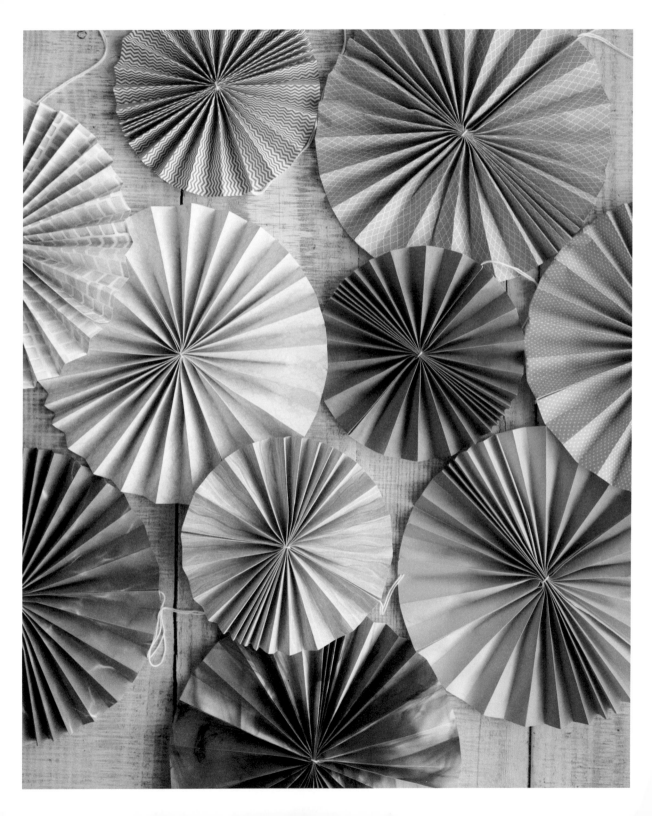

These instructions tell you how to make one fan, but the fans look great when hung in a group of six, seven, or more. Remember, you need three sheets of matching paper per fan, so shop accordingly.

Card stock is simply too thick for this project. Its thickness makes it hard to crease and makes the fans too bulky. Explore the scrapbooking section of your local craft store to find pretty papers to use.

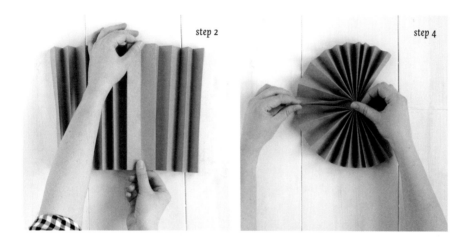

step 2

step 4

NAUTICAL ROPE NAPKIN KNOTS

•}}}❂{{{• •}}}❂{{{• •}}}❂{{{•

I first made these easy nautical napkin rings when my husband and I invited our supper club over for a summer seafood dinner several years ago. The materials are inexpensive, and the knots only take a few minutes to tie, but they add a wonderful maritime touch to the table. They casually hint at a nautical theme without being as literal as anchors and seashells.

MATERIALS & TOOLS:

28 inches (¼-inch) manila rope per napkin

Napkins and utensils

Sharp scissors

1. Lay out one section of the rope on a flat work surface.

2. Bundle up your napkins and utensils as you wish, and place one bundle on top of the rope section so that the rope runs behind the middle of the napkin.

3. Bring the right end of the rope over to the center of the napkin, and make a loop with the free end tucked behind the loop. You won't work with this side of the rope anymore. The rest of the knot-making all happens with the left half of the rope. Bring the left end of the rope over to the center of the napkin, and run it behind the right loop, over the end that stretches around to the back of the napkin, and under the free end. Then thread it over the front of the right loop, under itself, and then over the back of the right loop. If you get confused, refer to the pictures (see facing page), and remember that the left end of the rope goes over, under, over, under, and over.

4. Pull gently to tighten the knot slightly, then trim both free ends to about 2 inches. Gently pull the ends of the rope apart to fray them.

5. Repeat for the remaining napkin and utensil bundles.

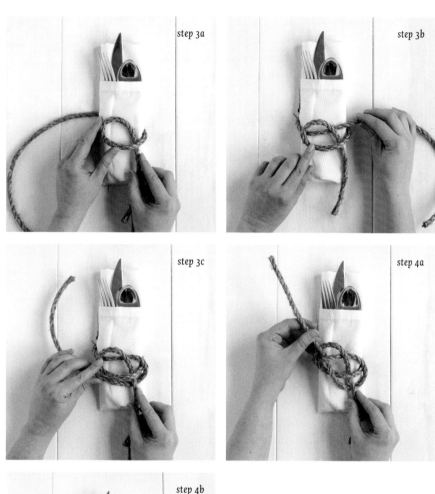

step 3a

step 3b

step 3c

step 4a

step 4b

Heritage Dinner

EACH OF THE SCANDINAVIAN COUNTRIES has a national day of celebration that looks a lot like the Fourth of July does in America. Homes and shops are draped with the national flag and decorated in its colors. Children dress up in traditional costumes and wave tiny flags in parades through the center of town. And friends and families gather to eat traditional foods. In my family we get together to celebrate Syttende Mai, or May 17, Norway's national day. My grandparents decorate their house with every Norwegian (and sometimes every Swedish!) thing they own.

CREATING THE GATHERING

If you have any national paraphernalia from a Scandinavian country—flag toothpicks, Ikea napkins, candlestick holders . . . anything!—this is the gathering at which to use them. Flower arrangements in the national colors should adorn the tables, on top of a tablecloth that's also in one of the national colors. If you have flags, hang them in front of your house, stick them in flower arrangements, or tuck them into place settings. And for an extra fun touch (I'm borrowing this tip from my mom and sister), find some Nordic folk music online and play it in the background during dinner!

RECIPES

Swedish Meatballs with Gravy
Danish Marinated Cucumber Salad (Agurksalat)
Finnish New Potatoes with Butter & Dill
Norwegian Rice Pudding (Riskrem)

PROJECTS

Paper Flag Garland
Painted Flag Place Mats

SWEDISH MEATBALLS WITH GRAVY

•}}}❂{{{• •}}}❂{{{• •}}}❂{{{•

Swedish meatballs might be the most iconic Scandinavian meal in the world. They are sold at every summer Scandinavian folk festival, are served at Nordic community dinners all over North America, and are as much a reason to go to Ikea as the affordable home goods. And they have all the hallmarks we expect from good comfort food: savory, rich, and belly warming.

**MAKES 3 DOZEN
1½-INCH MEATBALLS**

1 tablespoon extra-
　virgin olive oil
1 cup finely minced
　onion (from about
　1 small onion)
½ cup whole milk
½ cup Panko bread
　crumbs
1½ pounds ground beef
½ pound ground pork
2 eggs
2 tablespoons flour
1½ teaspoons table salt
⅛ teaspoon ground
　allspice
Freshly ground black
　pepper

For the gravy:
2 tablespoons butter
⅓ cup flour
4 cups low-sodium
　beef broth
¾ cup sour cream
Table salt and freshly
　ground black pepper
Finely chopped fresh
　parsley, for garnish

1. Preheat the oven to 350 degrees F.

2. In a large skillet over medium heat, heat the oil. Add the onions and sauté them until soft and translucent, about 5 minutes. Scoop the onions out, and set them on a small plate to cool.

3. In a large bowl, combine the milk and bread crumbs. Let it sit for 5 minutes.

4. Crumble the ground beef and pork into the bowl containing the milk and bread crumbs. Add the eggs, flour, salt, allspice, pepper to taste, and the sautéed onions. Mix gently until the ingredients are evenly distributed.

5. Form the mixture into 1½-inch balls. Working in batches, in the skillet over medium heat, sauté the meatballs until they are browned on all sides, about 2 minutes per side. Put the browned meatballs on a rimmed baking sheet.

6. When all of the meatballs are browned, put the baking sheet in the oven and bake until the meatballs are cooked through, about 10 minutes.

7. While the meatballs are baking, make the gravy. In the skillet used to brown the meatballs, melt the butter. Whisk in the flour and cook for 1 minute. Whisk in the beef broth, bring it to a simmer, and cook until the mixture is thickened, 4 to 5 minutes. Add the sour cream and cook for 8 to 10 minutes more. Add the salt and pepper to taste.

8. When the meatballs are done cooking, add them to the gravy, stir, and serve topped with parsley and a dollop of lingonberry jam on the side.

Lingonberry jam (see page 207 for more on lingonberry jam), for serving

DANISH MARINATED CUCUMBER SALAD (AGURKSALAT)

•⟫⟩❂⟨⟨• •⟫⟩❂⟨⟨• •⟫⟩❂⟨⟨•

I love using English cucumbers in this sweet and tangy traditional Scandinavian salad because the dark green of their skin adds a pop of pretty color. English cucumbers have thinner skins than traditional cucumbers, and they aren't typically waxed like traditional cucumber skins, so you don't have to peel them before slicing. They're usually wrapped in plastic in the produce section.

1. In a medium bowl, put the cucumbers and onions. Sprinkle with the salt and pepper.

2. In a small bowl, combine the water, vinegar, and sugar. Pour the dressing over the cucumber and onions and toss lightly.

3. Cover the bowl and refrigerate until the cucumbers and onions are chilled through.

4. Just before serving, garnish with the parsley.

MAKES 6 SERVINGS

2 large English
   cucumbers,
   thinly sliced
1 small sweet onion,
   peeled and
   thinly sliced
Pinch of table salt
Pinch of freshly ground
   black pepper
⅓ cup water
⅓ cup white vinegar
⅓ cup sugar
Chopped fresh flat-leaf
   parsley, for garnish

NATIONAL DAYS OF CELEBRATION

Norway: Syttende Mai (Seventeenth of May), May 17

Sweden: Sveriges Nationaldag (Swedish National Day), June 6

Denmark: Grundlovsdag (Constitution Day), June 5

Finland: Itsenäisyyspäivä (Independence Day), December 6

FINNISH NEW POTATOES WITH BUTTER & DILL

•⟩⟩⟩✿⟨⟨⟨• •⟩⟩⟩✿⟨⟨⟨• •⟩⟩⟩✿⟨⟨⟨•

These bite-size potatoes covered in butter and fresh dill couldn't be simpler, or a more perfect partner for Swedish Meatballs with Gravy (page 104). In early summer, when potatoes are new and just ready to harvest, they're a Scandinavian dinner table staple.

MAKES 6 SERVINGS

2¼ pounds baby
   or new potatoes
3 tablespoons butter
1½ tablespoons minced
   fresh baby dill
Table salt and freshly
   ground black pepper

1. In a large pot over high heat, cover the potatoes with cold water. Bring the potatoes to a boil, and cook until tender, 10 to 15 minutes. The time will depend on the size of the potatoes: the smaller they are, the more quickly they will cook.

2. When the potatoes are tender, drain the water out of the pot. Add the butter and baby dill, and the salt and pepper to taste. Toss until evenly distributed and serve.

NORWEGIAN RICE PUDDING (RISKREM)

When I was a child, I ate dinner at a distant cousin's house at Christmastime and had rice pudding for dessert, a long-standing Scandinavian holiday tradition. Even now I can see those colored Christmas lights and the giant plastic candy cane filled with chocolates and treats—the prize for whichever lucky child found a whole almond hidden in their rice pudding. I also very clearly remember that I did not go home with that plastic candy cane. I think every serving of rice pudding should have an almond hidden in the bottom so that everyone wins! Make sure to only use medium-grain white rice for this recipe to ensure a smooth custard with plump, tender grains of rice.

MAKES 6 SERVINGS

1 cup cooked medium-grain white rice (like Calrose)
½ cup raisins or dried, sweetened cranberries
2 cups whole milk
1 tablespoon butter
2 eggs
½ cup sugar
1 teaspoon vanilla extract
Pinch of table salt
Lightly sweetened whipped cream, for topping (optional)
Cinnamon, cinnamon sugar, or nutmeg, for topping (optional)
Whole almonds, for serving

Special equipment:
Fine mesh sieve

1. Preheat the oven to 350 degrees F. Spray an 8-by-8-inch glass pan or a 2-quart baking dish with nonstick cooking spray. Put a large kettle of water on to boil.

2. Spread the rice evenly in the bottom of the baking dish, and top with the raisins.

3. In a small saucepan over medium-low heat, cook the milk and butter until small bubbles form at the edges of the milk and the butter is completely melted.

4. In a medium bowl, whisk together the eggs, sugar, vanilla, and salt. While whisking, slowly add the milk a little at a time and whisk until combined. Pour the milk mixture through a fine mesh sieve and into the baking dish.

5. Put a large roasting pan in the oven and put the baking dish in it. Pour boiling water from the kettle into the roasting pan, *but not into the pan with the rice pudding in it.* Pour in enough water that it comes up the sides of the rice pudding pan 1 inch. Bake for 30 minutes, until a knife inserted in the center of the pudding comes out clean. It's okay if the pudding is still jiggly; it'll set up more as it cools. Allow it to cool slightly before serving. Serve plain or topped with the whipped cream and a sprinkle of cinnamon. Be sure to hide a whole almond at the bottom of each person's dish!

PAPER FLAG GARLAND

•}}}❂{{{• •}}}❂{{{• •}}}❂{{{•

Scandinavians love their national flags! They are the main decoration on most holidays—hung outside homes and shops, waved by costumed children in parades, and draped across mantels and Christmas trees during the holiday season. These homemade flag garlands, with their mix of shapes and patterns, are even cuter than the plain paper garlands you can find in Scandinavian stores. They are a darling addition to heritage celebrations, Christmas trees, birthday presents, packages, and dinner tables.

MATERIALS & TOOLS:

Photocopier or scanner/printer

Paper Flag Garland template (pages 220 to 223)

White card stock

Scissors

1- to 2-inch paper punches in various shapes (plain circles, scalloped circles, hearts, etc.)

Small single-hole paper punch

Baker's twine or string, plain white or striped

Thin clear tape

1. Photocopy or scan the flag garland template, and print it out on white card stock. You may need more than one sheet depending on how long you want your garland to be.

2. Cut out rectangular flags using scissors. Trim the end farthest from the cross into a notch. Use paper punches to punch out circles and hearts if desired.

3. Lay out all the shapes and arrange them in the order and direction you want them to be in the garland. Leave about ¼ inch of space between shapes. Use a single-hole punch to punch two holes in the top edge of each shape.

4. Cut a piece of baker's twine that extends past the shapes 12 inches on each end. String the paper shapes onto the string, putting the string through the first hole from front to back, and pulling the string back through the second hole from back to front. This way, the string runs behind each piece of paper and not across the front.

5. Make sure the spacing between shapes is still ¼ inch, then put a small piece of tape over the string on the back of each shape to hold it in place on the garland.

6. Hang your garland and enjoy!

PAINTED FLAG PLACE MATS

•⟩⟩⟩✪⟨⟨⟨• •⟩⟩⟩✪⟨⟨⟨• •⟩⟩⟩✪⟨⟨⟨•

Place mats make it easy to set an elegant table without getting out and ironing your special-occasion tablecloth. These hand-painted place mats resemble Scandinavian flags and add a chic, effortless style to your dinner party. The technique is simple: use painter's tape to isolate the areas to be painted and add layers of color to create a flag design.

FOR THE NORWEGIAN FLAG:

1. Lay out a place mat on a flat work surface. Use the measuring tape to measure the width of the place mat and make a small pencil mark one-third of the way across. This is the center of your vertical stripe. Measure the height of the place mat, and make a small pencil mark exactly halfway up. This is the center of your horizontal stripe.

2. Place two pieces of tape on the place mat vertically, the first 1½ inches to the left of the pencil mark, the second 1½ inches to the right. The space between them should be 3 inches wide. Place two pieces of tape on the place mat horizontally, the first 1½ inches above the pencil mark, the second 1½ inches below. Using the scissors, carefully cut out the places where the tape strips overlap so that you have a large cross on your place mat. Using the sponge brush, paint the area between the pieces of tape red. After you are done painting, remove the tape before the paint dries. Allow the paint to dry completely before moving on.

3. Repeat step 2, placing all of the tape pieces ½ inch closer to the center of the stripes than before. The space between them should be 2 inches wide. Paint the area between the tape white. Leave the tape in place this time, allow the paint to dry, then paint another coat. Remove the tape and allow the paint to dry completely before moving on.

CONTINUED

MATERIALS & TOOLS:

Natural, tan, or oatmeal-colored cloth place mats

Measuring tape or ruler

Pencil

1-inch-wide painter's tape

Small, sharp scissors

Sponge brush

Fabric paint (see page 208 for exact colors used in the Norwegian flag pictured on page 113)

> For the Norwegian flag: red, white, and navy blue

> For the Swedish flag: sky blue and sunshine yellow

> For the Danish flag: red and white

> For the Finnish flag: white and royal blue

Clean rag, pillowcase, or pressing cloth

Ironing board

Iron

step 2a

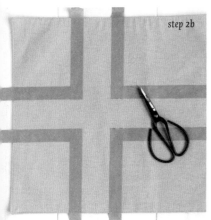

step 2b

4. Repeat step 3, placing all of the tape pieces ½ inch closer to the center of the stripes than before. The space between them should be 1 inch wide. Paint the area between the tape blue. As soon as you are done painting, remove the tape and allow the paint to dry completely. Repeat with the remaining place mats.

5. When the place mats are completely dry, cover them with a clean rag, pillowcase, or pressing cloth, and press them with a hot iron on the cotton setting, no steam, to set the paint. Launder gently and only as needed. Spot clean when possible.

FOR THE SWEDISH FLAG:

1. Lay out a place mat on a flat work surface. Use the measuring tape to measure the width of the place mat and make a small pencil mark one-third of the way across. This is the center of your vertical stripe. Measure the height of the place mat, and make a small pencil mark exactly halfway up. This is the center of your horizontal stripe.

2. Place two pieces of tape on the place mat vertically, the first 1 inch to the left of the pencil mark, the second 1 inch to the right. The space between them should be 2 inches wide. Place two pieces of tape on the place mat horizontally, the first 1 inch above the pencil mark, the second 1 inch below. Using the scissors, carefully cut out the places where the tape strips overlap so that you have a large cross on your place mat. Using the sponge brush, paint the area between the pieces of tape sky blue. After you are done painting, remove the tape before the paint dries. Allow the paint to dry completely before moving on.

3. Repeat step 2, placing all of the tape pieces ½ inch closer to the center of the stripes than before. The space between them should be 1 inch wide. Paint the area between the tape yellow. Leave the tape in place this time, allow the paint to dry, then paint another coat. Remove the tape and allow the paint to dry completely before moving on.

4. When the place mats are completely dry, cover them with a clean rag, pillowcase, or pressing cloth, and press them with a hot iron on the cotton setting, no steam, to set the paint. Launder gently and only as needed. Spot clean when possible.

FOR THE DANISH FLAG:

1. Repeat the steps for the Swedish flag using red paint for step 2 and white paint for step 3.

FOR THE FINNISH FLAG:

1. Repeat the steps for the Swedish flag using white paint for step 2 and royal-blue paint for step 3.

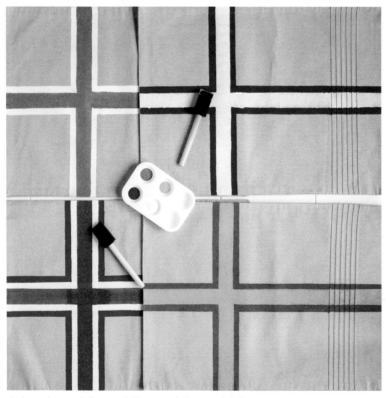

clockwise from top left: Finnish flag, Danish flag, Swedish flag, Norwegian flag

Lucia Day

ON THE THIRTEENTH OF DECEMBER, when the darkness of the year
is growing ever longer, this celebration of light is most welcome. Cities
and towns throughout Scandinavia (and American cities with large
Scandinavian populations) hold Lucia festivals filled with music and
candlelight. The main attraction is always the Lucia procession, featuring
a girl clad in a long white gown with a red sash and wearing an evergreen
crown with towering candles. In family celebrations at home, one of the
daughters dresses up as Lucia and serves her family coffee, gingersnaps,
and saffron buns before the sun rises. Lucia Day reminds us of light and
generosity, even in the darkness of midwinter.

CREATING THE GATHERING

Lucia Day is traditionally a simple holiday. It isn't ever meant to compete with or overshadow Christmas. Fresh evergreen branches instead of flower arrangements make the house look and smell fantastic. Since the holiday is a celebration of light, clusters of glowing candles sit atop white tablecloths, and store-bought paper lanterns shaped like stars hang from windows and light fixtures. Serve *pepparkakor* and lucia buns with coffee and cider for a casual Lucia Day celebration.

RECIPES

Spiced Cider
Sugared Gingersnaps (Swedish Pepparkakor)
Lucia Buns (Swedish Lussekatter)

PROJECTS

Candlelit Evergreen Lucia Table Wreath
Paint-Dipped Pinecone Garland
Tiny Star Wall Hanging

SPICED CIDER

•)))✪(((• •)))✪(((• •)))✪(((•

I'm lucky enough to be married to a fantastic cook! One of the many delicious recipes he brought to our marriage is his family's spiced cider recipe. We begin making it as soon as the weather turns brisk in the fall, and continue to enjoy it until warmth and sunshine return in the spring. This cider—deeply flavorful and full of citrus and spice—is a nonalcoholic version of *glögg*, a hot, spiced wine drink beloved in Scandinavia on Lucia Day and throughout the winter months.

MAKES ABOUT 1 GALLON

1 gallon apple cider or
    apple juice
1 (12-ounce) can frozen
    apple juice concentrate
½ (12-ounce) can
    frozen orange juice
    concentrate
2 teaspoons whole
    allspice
2 teaspoons whole cloves
2 to 3 cinnamon sticks
Dash of ground cinnamon

1. In a large pot over medium heat, combine all the ingredients. Bring the cider to a simmer.

2. Reduce the heat to low, and allow the cider to steep for 1 hour. Strain off the whole spices before serving, and serve hot.

3. Leftovers can be stored, covered, in the refrigerator and reheated as needed.

SUGARED GINGERSNAPS (SWEDISH PEPPARKAKOR)

•))) ❉ (((• •))) ❉ (((• •))) ❉ (((•

It's a good thing that both ginger and molasses have healthful properties, because these cookies are completely irresistible! They are deliciously crisp on the edges, with just a hint of chewiness in the middle. They have the perfect amount of warm spiciness without being harsh or hot. But my favorite thing about them is the crunchy coating of coarse sugar that makes them sparkle.

**MAKES ABOUT
3½ DOZEN GINGERSNAPS**

2 cups plus 1 tablespoon
    flour
2 teaspoons ground
    ginger
1½ teaspoons baking
    soda
1 teaspoon ground
    cinnamon
½ teaspoon ground
    cardamom
½ teaspoon ground
    cloves
1 cup lightly packed light
    brown sugar
¼ teaspoon table salt
10 tablespoons butter,
    softened
¼ cup molasses
1 egg
1 teaspoon vanilla extract
Coarse sugar,
    for sprinkling

Special equipment:
Parchment paper,
    for rolling and baking
2- to 2½-inch round
    cookie cutter

1. In a medium bowl, combine the flour, ginger, baking soda, cinnamon, cardamom, cloves, and salt. Set aside.

2. In a large bowl with an electric mixer or in the bowl of a stand mixer fitted with the paddle attachment, beat the brown sugar and butter on medium speed until fluffy, about 1 minute. Add the molasses, egg, and vanilla, and beat on medium speed until smooth, scraping the sides and bottom of the bowl with a rubber spatula as necessary.

3. With the mixer on low speed, gradually add the dry ingredients, beating just until combined.

4. Divide the dough into two equal portions. Lay each portion of the dough on a piece of parchment paper generously sprinkled with flour. Sprinkle the top of the dough with more flour, and cover it with another piece of parchment paper. Roll each ball of dough out between its two pieces of parchment paper, to a thickness of ¼ inch. Stack both pieces of rolled dough on a baking sheet, and refrigerate until firm, at least 1 hour.

5. Preheat the oven to 350 degrees F. Prepare baking sheets by lining them with clean parchment paper or silicone baking mats.

6. Remove one portion of chilled dough from the refrigerator and remove the top sheet of parchment paper. Cut out the cookies using a 2- to 2½-inch round cookie cutter. Using a thin spatula, gently place the cookies on the prepared baking sheets, leaving several inches between cookies. You can roll leftover dough scraps into a ball and roll them back out between floured

parchment sheets as mentioned in step 4, and cut out more cookies. The dough softens very quickly and becomes hard to work with. If it gets too soft, put it back in the refrigerator until it firms up. Meanwhile, you can work with the other chilled portion of dough.

7. Sprinkle the cookies with the coarse sugar, and bake them for 10 minutes. When the cookies are done, they will be puffed and look dry; they will flatten as they cool.

8. Remove the baking sheets from the oven and allow the cookies to cool on the baking sheets for 2 to 3 minutes before placing the cookies on a cooling rack to cool completely. Store leftovers in an airtight container. I think they are crispier and taste even better on day two!

Scandinavian gingersnaps come in all kinds of shapes: stars, hearts, gingerbread people, pine trees, reindeer . . . basically any fun Christmas shape you can think of. For this particular recipe, however, circles end up looking the best. These cookies puff up as they bake, then flatten out as they cool, which makes other shapes look distorted. But the circles look consistently beautiful, and every bit as authentic.

Gingersnaps are a very traditional holiday cookie in Scandinavia, especially on Lucia Day. They are known as *pepparkakor* in Sweden, *piparkakut* in Finnish, *pepperkaker* in Norwegian, and *brunkager* (literally *brown biscuits*) in Danish. In Astrid Lindgren's beloved novel *Pippi Longstocking*, the whimsical heroine Pippi decides to make five hundred gingersnaps one morning, and rolls them out on the floor—the only place big enough to accommodate that many cookies!

LUCIA BUNS (SWEDISH LUSSEKATTER)

•}}}❁{{{• •}}}❁{{{• •}}}❁{{{•

Early in the morning on Lucia Day, the oldest daughter in the family serves her parents and siblings coffee and these tasty Swedish pastries. With their slightly sweet flavor, light texture, and golden color, I can see why this delicious tradition has lasted for hundreds of years!

MAKES 18 ROLLS

½ gram saffron
1 cup whole milk
1 tablespoon active
　dry yeast
⅓ cup sugar, plus a pinch
　for proofing the yeast
3½ cups flour
½ cup sour cream
1 teaspoon table salt
4 tablespoons butter,
　softened
1 egg
1 tablespoon water
36 dried, sweetened
　cranberries
Swedish pearl sugar
　(optional, but so good—
　see page 207 for
　more on pearl sugar),
　for sprinkling

1. On a small plate, grind the saffron with the back of a spoon until it is powdered. If you have a mortar and pestle, that will work wonderfully.

2. In a small saucepan over medium-low heat, heat the milk until just beginning to simmer. Remove the pan from the heat, add the saffron, and stir. Allow the mixture to cool to the temperature of a warm bath. When the milk is warm but not hot, add the yeast and a pinch of the sugar. Allow the mixture to sit until it is bubbling and has grown in volume, about 5 minutes (see page xix for tips on making yeast breads).

3. While the yeast mixture is proofing, in a large bowl with a wooden spoon or in the bowl of a stand mixer fitted with the dough hook attachment, combine the sugar, flour, sour cream, and salt.

4. Add the yeast mixture, and knead until the dough is nice and smooth, and pulls away from the sides of the bowl.

5. Add the butter, 1 tablespoon at a time, and continue kneading the dough until it again pulls away from the sides of the bowl. It might seem like this is never going to happen, but all of a sudden, you'll have a nice, smooth ball of dough.

6. Put the dough in a lightly oiled bowl, cover with plastic wrap, and allow it to rise until doubled in size.

7. Punch down the risen dough, knead it briefly on a lightly floured counter, and divide the dough into eighteen equal portions.

CONTINUED

step 8a

step 8b

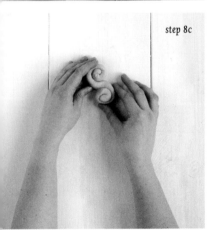

step 8c

8. Roll each piece of dough into a long, skinny strip, about 12 inches long. Roll the left end of the dough up and clockwise until it reaches the middle, then roll the right end down and clockwise until it reaches the middle. Your dough should now look like a very tightly rolled S.

9. Place the Ss on a parchment-lined baking sheet, cover with plastic wrap, and allow them to rise for 30 minutes.

10. Preheat the oven to 400 degrees F. While the buns are rising, in a small bowl, whisk together the egg and water. Just before baking, lightly brush the tops and sides of each lucia bun with the egg wash, place a cranberry at the center of each swirl, and sprinkle the tops with pearl sugar.

11. Bake the lucia buns for 8 minutes, or until they are puffed and golden. Remove the baking sheet from the oven and allow the buns to cool. Store leftovers in an airtight container.

Saffron can be expensive, but it gives these buns a unique flavor and beautiful golden color, so while you don't need much, it is a really important ingredient. I wait to buy saffron until the spices at my local grocery store are on sale, and I store it in the refrigerator to keep it fresh longer.

If you don't care for the flavor of saffron, this dough still makes delicious, all-purpose rolls. Just leave out the saffron!

CANDLELIT EVERGREEN LUCIA TABLE WREATH

The most iconic part of Lucia Day is Lucia's evergreen headdress with its towering candles aglow. Nowadays, the real candles in Lucia's crown have largely been replaced with battery-operated ones for the sake of safety; flaming candles on a young girl's head sound like a recipe for trouble! But a Lucia crown with real taper candles makes a beautiful centerpiece for a holiday gathering, bringing its soft glow to your celebration of light.

1. Put the wooden wreath form on a flat work surface. Place the candle cups on the wreath form, spreading them out evenly. If needed, you can use a ruler or measuring tape to help you place the candle cups. My wreath form had eight holes predrilled in it, so I placed each candle cup on top of a predrilled hole.

2. Glue each candle cup in place with a small amount of wood glue on the bottom of the candle cup. Allow the glue to dry completely before moving on.

3. Working outside or in a well-ventilated area, put garbage bags or newspaper on the ground to protect it from paint. A protected area about 4 by 4 feet should be big enough. Put the wreath form on the center of the garbage bags, and spray it with the paint following the application directions on the spray-paint can. Add as many coats as necessary (one to two), and allow the wreath form to dry completely.

4. When the paint is dry, add the garland to the wreath. Place one end of the garland on the wreath form between two candle cups. Use about 10 inches of green floral wire wrapped around the garland and wreath form to hold the garland firmly in place. Gently weave the greenery between the candle cups, passing the garland outside one candle cup, then inside the next. Where the garland crosses the wreath form between candle cups, wire it in place. Make two complete circles around the wreath. On the second time around, go on the opposite side of each cup so that the candle cups are completely surrounded.

MATERIALS & TOOLS:

12-inch wooden wreath form

8 large 1-inch wood candle cups

Ruler or measuring tape (optional)

Wood glue

Newspaper or clean garbage bags

Dark-green spray paint that blends in with your garland

12 feet of small-leaved greenery garland, real or faux (I used faux boxwood garland)

Thin green floral wire

Wire cutters

8 taper candles that fit your candle cups

CONTINUED

5. When you've completed two full circles, wire the end of the garland in place. Use the wire cutters to cut small sections of the remaining garland (2 or 3 inches long), and tuck them into the centerpiece to make it fuller and cover any bare spots or wires that are visible.

6. Fit the tapers into the candle cups, and place on the table.

Candles should never be left unattended while burning. Replace the taper candles when they have burned down to within 2 inches of the greenery.

Lucia was not Scandinavian; she was actually a very young, very beautiful Sicilian martyr in the early Christian church. How she came to be associated with a celebration of light in the middle of the Scandinavian winter remains a mystery, and seems to be a muddle of ancient Norse folklore and Italian history.

The Lucia procession is led by Lucia, wearing a long white gown, a red sash, and her iconic evergreen crown with glowing candles. Her attendants follow behind her. They wear similar dresses minus the red sash and candle crown. Next come the star boys, also dressed in white, wearing tall pointed white caps and carrying long wands with golden stars on the ends. Santa sometimes makes an appearance in the Lucia processions, and the *tomten* or *nisser*, the mischievous little pixies, bring up the rear. Everyone carries a candle in their hands, and sings the Lucia song (which was originally a Neapolitan gondolier song).

PAINT-DIPPED PINECONE GARLAND

•))}❂(((• •))}❂(((• •))}❂(((•

When I think of Scandinavia during the holidays, I think of cozy, light-filled houses sur-rounded by quiet, snowy forests—basically a dreamy midwinter fairy tale. The bit of white paint on the tips of these pinecones makes them look like they've been dusted with snow. Hung from a mantel, over a doorway, or across the top of a piano, they bring the beauty of a wintry Nordic forest to hearth and home.

MATERIALS & TOOLS:

Small eye screws,
1 per pinecone

Pinecones

White acrylic craft paint
(see page 208 for
exact color)

Paper plate, cardboard,
or something to put the
paint on

Thick jute twine

Scissors

This garland is fun to make using pinecones that have been foraged or gathered from nearby parks or neighborhoods, or from your own backyard. Just make sure the pinecones are sturdy, completely dried out, and bug free before using.

1. Gently screw an eye screw into the top of each pinecone. Push firmly down on the screw while twisting it until it catches, then twist it into the pinecone until it is tight. If you just can't get the screw to go into the pinecone, gently tap it in with a hammer until it catches, then twist it in until tight.

2. Squirt some white paint onto a piece of cardboard, and spread it into a thin layer.

3. Roll the pinecones through the paint so that just the edges pick up a touch of white. Set the pinecones aside to dry completely.

4. Lay out the dry painted pinecones in a line, leaving about 3 inches between each pinecone. Use the scissors to cut a piece of twine that extends past your pinecone 24 inches on each side. Thread the first pinecone onto the twine using the eye screw. Move it 12 inches from the far end of the twine, and tie a knot around the eye screw to secure it in place.

5. Thread another pinecone onto the twine. Move it just over 3 inches from the previous pinecone, and tie a knot around the eye screw to secure it in place.

6. Continue adding pinecones by repeating step 5 until all pine-cones have been tied onto the twine. If more than 12 inches of twine is left over after the last pinecone is tied on, trim the end of the twine to a length of 12 inches.

TINY STAR WALL HANGING

•}})✪{{{• •}})✪{{{• •}})✪{{{•

These delicate white hanging stars are easy to make in bulk, and they look beautiful clustered together in a window or hanging on the wall over a kitchen table.

1. Unwrap a package of oven-bake clay, place it on a smooth, hard surface, and use the rolling pin to roll it out to a thickness of about ⅛ inch.

2. Use the cookie cutter to cut fifteen clay stars.

3. Use the spatula to gently lift the stars off the work surface.

4. Use the bamboo skewer or chopstick to poke a hole through each star (in the center, about ¼ inch from the top).

5. Place the stars on a clean baking sheet, and bake according to package directions.

6. Remove the baking sheet from the oven and allow the stars to cool completely.

7. Cut the white thread into various lengths between 18 and 24 inches. Pass each piece of thread through the hole in a star, and secure it with a double knot.

8. Attach the stars to the twig or branch, being sure to vary the lengths of thread. Loop each piece of thread around the branch and double knot it to secure it in place. Space the stars evenly along the length of the branch.

9. Attach an eye screw to the top-left and top-right ends of the twig. Attach each end of the 24-inch length of twine to an eye screw.

MATERIALS & TOOLS:

2 packages of white
    oven-bake clay
Rolling pin or clay roller
Star-shaped cookie
    cutter, about
    1 inch wide
Thin metal spatula
Bamboo skewer or
    chopstick
Baking sheet
White all-purpose thread
Large twig or small tree
    branch, about 15 inches
    long and 1 inch in
    diameter
2 small eye screws
24 inches jute twine

Christmas Cookie Exchange

WHEN I THINK OF SCANDINAVIAN baking, the first thing that comes to mind is Christmas cookies. The Nordic people seem to have a knack for combining butter, sugar, and flour to make holiday treats that delight the taste buds. It is traditional among Scandinavian families to make no fewer than seven different types of cookies during the holiday season. That sounds like a good excuse for a Christmas cookie exchange to me!

CREATING THE GATHERING

Make sure your Christmas tree is already up and decorated, and trim your house with paper chains and heart garlands. Red and white are perfect colors for a Scandinavian Christmas cookie exchange, and pink and turquoise add fun pops of candy-hued color. If you can find white poinsettia or white amaryllis, wrap their pots in white butcher paper with big bows tied around them in red, pink, and turquoise, and decorate your front porch and party area with them. When you send out invitations for your cookie exchange, ask guests to bring four dozen of their favorite holiday cookies with them, and make four dozen of your favorite too. Tell guests to bring two plates of two-dozen cookies each, so that when they arrive, half of the cookies can be set aside to exchange at the end of the party. Fold a stack of blank three-by-five-inch index cards in half widthwise and have a nice pen handy so that guests can make a little sign for their cookies as they arrive. Have lots of small plates and napkins so guests can eat their fill of delicious holiday cookies during the party, and have a stack of mugs or paper hot cups at the ready for homemade hot chocolate. When the end of the party is drawing nigh, bring out the reserved cookies and allow guests to fill their take-home boxes with an assortment of their favorites.

RECIPES

Waffle Cookies
Spiced Oatmeal Cookies with Dried Cherries & Almonds
Chocolate-Dipped Almond Horns
Jam Cakes (Swedish Syltkakor)
Hot Chocolate with Homemade Cardamom Marshmallows

PROJECTS

Mini Danish Heart Garland
Papier-Mâché Gingerbread Cookie Boxes
Colorful Cookie Pedestals

WAFFLE COOKIES

•}}}❂{{{• •}}}❂{{{• •}}}❂{{{•

I got this unique recipe a decade ago from my dear friend Marcelle. The recipe is a childhood favorite of her husband's, whose mom made them every Christmas for her family. To make your waffle cookies look truly Scandinavian, as Marcelle always does, use a traditional heart-shaped waffle iron. If you only have a regular square waffle iron, never fear; your cookies will be just as delicious!

1. Preheat a heart-shaped or standard waffle iron on the medium setting. A Belgian waffle iron will not work for these cookies.

2. In a large bowl with an electric mixer or in the bowl of a stand mixer fitted with the paddle attachment, cream the butter and sugars together on medium speed until light and fluffy, about 1 minute. Add the eggs one at a time, beating after each addition. Add the vanilla and mix until blended.

3. In a medium bowl, combine the flour and salt, and add the dry ingredients to the butter mixture. With an electric mixer, beat on low until a smooth dough forms, 20 to 30 seconds.

4. Roll the dough in 1-inch balls, and set the balls on a baking sheet.

5. Place one ball of dough on each heart or square on the waffle iron, and close the lid. Cook for 2 to 3 minutes, or until the waffle cookies are golden. If the waffle cookies are cooking too fast or too slowly, feel free to adjust the temperature setting on your waffle iron as needed.

6. Gently remove the cookies from the waffle iron using two forks—one on the bottom to gently lift the cookies, and one on the top to help steady them. Place the hot cookies on a cooling rack to cool completely.

CONTINUED

MAKES 3 TO 4 DOZEN 2½-INCH COOKIES

1 cup butter
1 cup granulated sugar
½ cup lightly packed light brown sugar
3 eggs
1 teaspoon vanilla extract
3 cups flour
½ teaspoon table salt

Special equipment:
Heart-shaped or standard waffle iron

7. Working in batches, continue making cookies until all of the batter is used up.

8. Store cooled cookies in an airtight container.

VARIATIONS:

• You can cut the vanilla called for in the recipe in half and substitute with almond, lemon, or orange extract, or maple flavoring. Use ½ teaspoon vanilla and ½ teaspoon of one of the extracts or flavorings listed.

Two common Christmas cookies in Norway are *goro*, or *rich man cookies*, and *fattigman*, or *poor man cookies*. *Goro* are cooked in a special cookie press, while *fattigman*, which have a similar ingredient list, are twisted and fried. I've seen *fattigman* called all sorts of other names. My grandpa calls them *bakkels*, while an acquaintance of my husband has brought them to us and called them Danish *klejner*. No matter the name, they are delicious!

SPICED OATMEAL COOKIES WITH DRIED CHERRIES & ALMONDS

•)))⦿(((• •)))⦿(((• •)))⦿(((•

Thin, lacy oatmeal cookies pop up often in my old Scandinavian cookbooks, but I have a soft spot for oatmeal cookies that are thick and chewy. I find them impossible to stay away from, especially warm and fresh from the oven. I gave my favorite oatmeal cookie recipe a Nordic holiday makeover by adding cardamom (considered the cinnamon of Scandinavia), tart dried cherries, and crunchy almonds. And if it's possible, I like them even better than the originals.

1. Preheat the oven to 350 degrees F and line three baking sheets with parchment paper.

2. In a large bowl with an electric mixer or in the bowl of a stand mixer fitted with the paddle attachment, cream the butter and sugars together on medium speed until light and fluffy, about 1 minute. Add the eggs one at a time, beating after each addition. Add the vanilla and mix until blended.

3. In a medium bowl, combine the flour, salt, baking soda, baking powder, cinnamon, and cardamom. Then add the dry ingredients to the butter-and-sugar mixture. Beat on low until combined.

4. Stir in the oats, cherries, and almonds. The dough might be too thick for an electric mixer at this point. If that's the case, stir in these last additions by hand with a wooden spoon.

5. Scoop the dough into 2-tablespoon balls (about the size of a Ping-Pong ball), and place them 2 inches apart on the prepared baking sheets. Place twelve cookie dough balls on each baking sheet.

6. Bake for 11 minutes, or until the cookies are set and slightly flattened out. Put the cookies on a cooling rack to finish cooling completely.

MAKES 3 DOZEN COOKIES

1 cup butter, softened
1 cup granulated sugar
1 cup lightly packed light brown sugar
2 eggs
1 teaspoon vanilla extract
2 cups flour
1 teaspoon table salt
1 teaspoon baking soda
1 teaspoon baking powder
1 teaspoon ground cinnamon
½ teaspoon ground cardamom
3 cups old-fashioned rolled oats
1 cup dried tart cherries
½ cup sliced almonds

Special equipment:
Parchment paper, for baking

CHOCOLATE-DIPPED ALMOND HORNS

•)}}◍{{{• •}}}◍{{{• •}}}◍{{{•

Almond paste and marzipan are both staples in Scandinavian baking. But while they're related, they aren't the same thing and are not interchangeable in recipes. Almond paste, an ingredient in these subtly sweet, crescent-shaped treats, is made from coarsely ground almonds and sugar, usually in equal proportions. It is a common ingredient in baked goods, especially in the almond-loving Nordic countries. Marzipan, on the other hand, usually contains much more sugar and is very smooth. It is sometimes called candy dough and is used mostly as a decoration, like those cute little painted fruit candies you see around the holidays. You can find the almond paste for this recipe in the baking aisle at your local grocery store, usually near the canned pie filling.

1. In a large bowl with an electric mixer or in the bowl of a stand mixer fitted with the paddle attachment, combine the almond paste, confectioners' sugar, butter, egg, orange zest, vanilla, almond extract, and salt. Beat on medium speed for 3 minutes, until fluffy and mostly smooth.

2. Add the flour and ¾ cup of the almonds, and beat on low speed just until the dough comes together. Cover the bowl with plastic wrap, and chill it for 1 hour.

3. Preheat the oven to 350 degrees F. Line two baking sheets with parchment paper or silicone baking mats.

4. Roll the chilled dough into 1-inch balls. Roll each ball into a cylinder about 2½ inches long, then bend each into a slight crescent shape and place it on a prepared baking sheet. Place the crescents several inches apart. You should be able to fit eighteen cookies per baking sheet.

5. Bake for 10 minutes, or until the cookies are set and just beginning to turn golden on the tips. Remove the baking sheet from the oven and allow the cookies to cool completely on a wire rack.

MAKES 3 DOZEN COOKIES

3½ ounces almond paste, crumbled
½ cup confectioners' sugar
½ cup butter
1 egg
1 tablespoon orange zest
1 teaspoon vanilla extract
¼ teaspoon almond extract
¼ teaspoon table salt
1¾ cups flour
1 cup finely chopped sliced almonds, divided
6 ounces semisweet chocolate

Special equipment:
Parchment paper, for baking

CONTINUED

6. When the cookies are cool, melt the chocolate in a small, microwave-safe bowl. Microwave the bowl in 30-second intervals, stirring after each one, until the chocolate is melted and smooth. Dip part of each cookie in the chocolate and return it to the lined baking sheet to allow the chocolate to set up. Sprinkle the chocolate-dipped edge of each cookie with the remaining ¼ cup almonds. Once all of the cookies have been dipped, you can put the baking sheets in the refrigerator for a few minutes to speed up the chocolate-setting process.

I have found that the most foolproof way to melt chocolate is to use chocolate that is intended for melting. Ghirardelli and Baker's both make melting/dipping chocolates that are easy to use and taste great. They can be found in the baking aisle at most large grocery stores, usually near the chocolate chips.

JAM CAKES (SWEDISH SYLTKAKOR)

•))}❁{{{• •))}❁{{{• •))}❁{{{•

Jam cakes are one of those recipes that every Scandinavian grandmother seems to have her own spin on. Some people make one long rectangle with jam down the center that is cut into thin slices after baking. Some people make thin, buttery sandwich cookies filled with sweet jam. Some people make what we in America know as thumbprint cookies. My personal favorite is represented here: a thumbprint cookie crossed with a tiny tea cake. The dollop of fruity jam in the center of these light, crumbly cakes adds a burst of interesting color and flavor. And their mini cake shape looks darling and unique on a holiday cookie table. Be sure to try the Nutella-filled variation too (see page 144); it is irresistible.

1. Preheat the oven to 325 degrees F. Line mini muffin tins with paper liners, and set aside.

2. In a large bowl with an electric mixer or in the bowl of a stand mixer fitted with the paddle attachment, combine the butter and sugar. Beat on medium speed until light and fluffy, about 1 minute. Add the egg yolk and vanilla, and beat until smooth, scraping down the sides and bottom of the bowl as necessary.

3. In a small bowl, combine the flour, baking powder, and salt. Add the dry ingredients to the butter-and-sugar mixture and beat on low speed just until the dough comes together.

4. Roll the dough into 1-inch balls, roll each ball in sugar, and place each ball in a mini muffin paper. Use the end of a wooden spoon to make a well in the center of each ball. Be careful not to make the well too deep; you don't want to poke a hole all the way through! If the spoon starts to stick, dip the end in flour first.

5. Spoon the jam into a small ziplock bag. Twist the bag shut (like you would a frosting bag when decorating a cake), snip off one bottom corner of the bag, and pipe a small amount of jam into the well of each ball of cookie dough. Fill the wells just to the top.

MAKES ABOUT 3½ DOZEN MINI MUFFIN-SIZE COOKIES

1 cup butter, softened
¾ cup sugar, plus more for rolling
1 egg yolk
1 tablespoon vanilla extract
2 cups flour
¾ teaspoon baking powder
¼ teaspoon table salt
Red raspberry jam

Special equipment:
Mini muffin tins
Paper liners

CONTINUED

6. Bake the cookies for 12 to 15 minutes, until the cookies are set but not yet beginning to brown. Allow the cookies to cool completely before removing them from the mini muffin tins.

VARIATIONS:

• You can use any flavor of jam you like. Raspberry jam's boldness is a particularly nice contrast to the sweet, buttery cookie base, and the deep-red color is stunning, but strawberry, apricot, and sour cherry preserves are tasty as well.

• For a nice change of pace, replace the jam filling with Nutella. In a small bowl, microwave the Nutella for 15 to 30 seconds before putting it in the bag and filling the cookies. At room temperature, it is sticky and hard to work with.

After cooling, the jam-filled cookies will sink slightly in the center. That's normal, so don't worry when it happens.

HOT CHOCOLATE WITH HOMEMADE CARDAMOM MARSHMALLOWS

•}}}❂{{{• •}}}❂{{{• •}}}❂{{{•

My family loves hot chocolate. Not the kind made with hot water and a paper envelope of hot cocoa mix, but the kind made from scratch with milk and melted chocolate. After years of delicious trial and error, we have finally hit upon the perfect homemade hot chocolate. Topped with my mother-in-law's sweet and lightly spiced cardamom marshmallows, it is a rich and delightful addition to any holiday party.

1. In a medium saucepan over medium-low heat, combine the milk, chocolates, condensed milk, and salt. Stir occasionally until the chocolate is melted and the beverage is hot, 25 to 30 minutes. Divide the hot chocolate into four mugs and serve with the marshmallows.

MAKES 4 SERVINGS

4 cups milk (anything but skim)
3½ ounces dark chocolate (around 70 percent cacao), chopped
3½ ounces milk chocolate (around 30 percent cacao), chopped
¼ cup sweetened condensed milk
Pinch of table salt
Cardamom Marshmallows (recipe follows)

Cardamom Marshmallows

**MAKES 9 TO 10 DOZEN
1-INCH SQUARE
MARSHMALLOWS**

3 packets unflavored
   gelatin
1 cup cold water, divided
2 cups sugar
½ cup light corn syrup
¼ teaspoon table salt
2 teaspoons vanilla
   extract
½ teaspoon ground
   cinnamon
¼ teaspoon ground
   cardamom
¼ cup confectioners'
   sugar
¼ cup cornstarch

Special equipment:
Candy thermometer
Sifter or fine mesh sieve

1. In a large bowl with an electric mixer or in the bowl of a stand mixer fitted with the whip attachment, sprinkle the gelatin over ½ cup cold water. Let it stand until all of the gelatin is fully dissolved.

2. Meanwhile, in a medium saucepan over medium heat, combine the remaining ½ cup cold water with the sugar, corn syrup, and salt. Whisk until the sugar is dissolved, then increase the heat to medium-high and allow the mixture to boil until it reaches 240 degrees F on a candy thermometer.

3. With the mixer on low speed, slowly pour the hot sugar syrup into the gelatin mixture. When all of the syrup has been added, turn the mixer up to high speed, and whip the mixture until it is thick and white and has increased in volume, about 12 minutes.

4. Turn off the mixer, add the vanilla, cinnamon, and cardamom, and whip 1 more minute until incorporated.

5. In a small bowl, combine the confectioners' sugar and cornstarch. Lightly spray a 9-by-13-inch baking pan with nonstick cooking spray, then use a sifter to sift the confectioners' sugar mixture over the pan to coat the bottom and sides. Spread the marshmallow mixture evenly in the pan, then sprinkle with more confectioners' sugar mixture.

6. Allow the marshmallows to sit uncovered at room temperature until firm, at least 3 hours. Cut the marshmallows into 1-inch squares with a paring knife, and dip the cut ends in the remaining confectioners' sugar mixture. Store in an airtight container.

This recipe makes a lot of marshmallows—way more than you could possibly use for your hot chocolate! Instead of cutting the recipe in half, package the extra marshmallows up in a cellophane bag tied with striped baker's twine, and give them as an easy holiday gift.

MINI DANISH HEART GARLAND

•))}⦿{{{• •))}⦿{{{• •))}⦿{{{•

When I was growing up, we had a much-loved craft book full of simple, old-fashioned paper crafts like birthday crowns, paper bag masks, and red-and-white woven heart baskets. These little heart baskets are called *julehjerter*, or *Christmas hearts* in Danish, and are a popular holiday craft, especially for kids—you might have even made them when you were in elementary school! The red and white colors are reminiscent of the Danish flag and typical of Scandinavian Christmas decorations. This sweet garland made of tiny *julehjerter* in soft, candy colors is easy to make and would look as darling on your mantel at Valentine's Day as it does at Christmas.

1. Use a pencil to trace the heart garland template onto a piece of plain white paper, then cut it out using the scissors.

2. Cut each piece of card stock in half lengthwise, then cut each piece in half lengthwise again so that you have four long, skinny pieces of card stock in each color.

3. With the flat edge of the template against the long side of a piece of card stock, trace the template as many times as it will fit. Cut out each traced shape.

4. On each cut-out piece, draw two 1⅝-inch-long lines from the flat edge toward the curved edge. Draw each one ½ inch from the side so that they divide the paper into equal thirds. Cut on the lines you just drew.

5. Take one white piece and one red piece and weave them together following the pattern in the pictures (see page 152). Start by placing the two pieces of card stock with their flat edges near each other at a 45-degree angle, with the red piece of card stock on the left and with the white piece on the right.

6. Take the top strip of white and thread it over the first red strip, under the middle red strip, and over the last red strip.

MATERIALS & TOOLS:

Mini Danish Heart Garland template (page 212)

Plain white paper

Pencil

Scissors

12-by-12-inch card stock in red, white, pink, and turquoise (1 sheet per color)

Ruler or measuring tape

Craft glue

Baker's twine or string

CONTINUED

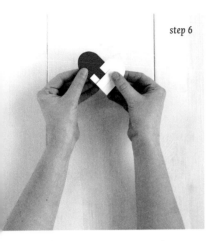

step 6

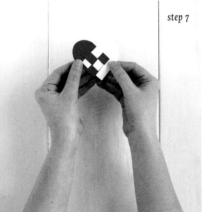

step 7

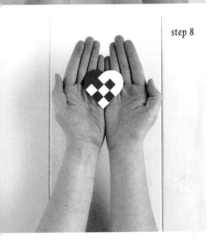

step 8

7. Next take the middle strip of white and thread it under the first red strip, over the middle red strip, and under the last red strip.

8. Finally, take the bottom strip of white and weave it just like you did the first white strip. Lightly glue any loose ends.

9. Repeat with red and white card stock, red and pink card stock, and red and turquoise card stock.

10. When all the hearts are woven together, lay them out on a flat work surface with about ½ inch between each heart, alternating red/white, red/pink, and red/turquoise hearts. If there are any pencil marks visible on the woven hearts, make sure they are face up; this will end up being the back of the garland. Lay out a piece of the twine or string that extends past the hearts about 12 inches on each side.

11. Put a thin line of glue across each heart about ¼ inch down from top edge. Lay the twine across the glue, and press firmly. Allow the glue to dry, then hang your garland!

PAPIER-MÂCHÉ GINGERBREAD COOKIE BOXES

One of the most important details of a cookie exchange—besides the cookies!—is a way for guests to pack up their sweet bounty and take it home. These papier-mâché boxes are easy to find at craft stores and look especially cute with some simple embellishment. Line them with squares of waxed paper and they're ready to be packed to the brim with holiday treats.

1. Take the lids off the papier-mâché boxes and set them aside. Use the white paint marker to decorate the boxes and lids like gingerbread houses. Don't go overboard; this is one of those times when less is more. You can see lots of design ideas in the photo (see below). Allow the marker to dry completely.

2. When the boxes are dry, place the lids on top.

MATERIALS & TOOLS:

Large round or square papier-mâché boxes with lids, 1 per guest

White water-based Sharpie paint marker

If you feel up to it, you can set up a station where guests can decorate their own cookie boxes. Be sure to have at least one extra box already decorated to give them some ideas of what to do. And remember that they are decorating their boxes the way *they* want to, not the way you want to!

COLORFUL COOKIE PEDESTALS

Presentation is everything when it comes to treats. These easy-to-create pedestals make cookies and treats look their best, and they are especially cute when grouped together on a dessert table. You can buy the plates and candlesticks needed at your local home goods store, or, for a fun, whimsical touch, look for mismatched plates and different sized candlesticks at thrift shops.

MATERIALS & TOOLS:

Newspaper or clean garbage bags

Small glass candlesticks with wide bases, 1 per pedestal

Spray paint in red, pink, and turquoise (see page 209 for exact colors)

Plain white dinner plates, 1 per pedestal

Strong adhesive, like E6000 or superglue

Ruler

1. Working outside or in a well-ventilated area, put garbage bags or newspaper on the ground to protect it from paint. A protected area about 4 by 4 feet should be big enough. Put a few of the candlesticks right side up on the center of the garbage bags, and spray them with red paint following the application directions on the spray-paint can. Add as many coats as necessary (one to two), and allow the candlesticks to dry completely. Repeat with more candlesticks and pink spray paint, then the remaining candlesticks and turquoise paint. Spray all of the red candlesticks in one area, all of the pink candlesticks in a second area, and all of the turquoise candlesticks in a third area so that each candlestick only has one color of paint on it.

2. When the candlesticks are completely dry, flip the plates over on a flat, level work surface. Put a thin layer of adhesive around the top rim of each candlestick, quickly flip it over, and stick it to the bottom of a plate right in the center. Use the ruler to make sure each candlestick is centered, and gently move any that are out of place. Allow the glue to dry completely (at least overnight, but 24 hours is even better) before using.

These cookie pedestals *cannot* go in the dishwasher. Gently wash them by hand, and always carry them with one hand on the candlestick and one hand under the plate.

Christmas Eve Supper

MY FAMILY GATHERS EVERY CHRISTMAS EVE for cozy soups, raspberry pudding with cream, and lots of Scandinavian tradition. For as long as I can remember, we have had Christmas Eve supper at Nana and Poppy's house. Every year, without fail, their house is beautifully dressed up in the traditional Scandinavian holiday manner: a tree covered in straw ornaments, white lights, and flag garlands; electric candles in every window; and Swedish angel chimes spinning gently on the top of the piano. It's one of my favorite parts of the Christmas season.

CREATING THE GATHERING

The traditional color palette of a Scandinavian Christmas is so beautiful: red and white accented by wheat and straw. Sticking with a limited color palette allows you to go over the top with decorating without looking like you did too much. If you have access to lovely Scandinavian table linens, especially in red with white stitching or accents, they would look especially festive on a Christmas Eve dinner table. Nana always sets her table with her Christmas china and gold-plated utensils, but nice white plates and bowls with your best flatware are sufficient if you don't have a well-stocked nana. Red poinsettias and amaryllis with their pots wrapped in kraft paper or burlap add a beautiful floral touch to the gathering. And candles in every nook and cranny will create a cozy atmosphere.

RECIPES

Split Pea Soup with Ham & Potatoes
Red Leaf Lettuce Salad with Raspberry-Citrus Vinaigrette & Sugared Almonds
Nana's Savory Multigrain Herb Bread
Raspberry Pudding with Cream (Danish Rødgrød med Flød)
Tante Kari's Hot Almond-Citrus Punch

PROJECTS

Hand-Stamped Wrapping Paper
Wheat Wreaths
Straw Star Ornaments

SPLIT PEA SOUP WITH HAM & POTATOES

•}}}❂{{{• •}}}❂{{{• •}}}❂{{{•

For as long as I can remember, my family has eaten soup for dinner on Christmas Eve. Nordic tradition calls for pea soup to be served for dinner on Thursdays, but this hearty, soul-satisfying Scandinavian favorite makes an excellent addition to the Christmas Eve dinner table. It seems tailor-made for dark winter nights.

1. In a large pot, combine the peas, chicken stock, water, thyme, and bay leaves. Bring it to a boil over medium heat, cover, reduce the heat to a simmer, and cook for 45 minutes.

2. While the peas are simmering, in a medium skillet over medium heat, sauté the onions, carrots, and celery in oil until the onions are translucent, 7 to 8 minutes. Add the garlic and cook 1 minute more.

3. Add the sautéed veggies and potatoes to the split peas. Simmer, covered, until tender, 20 to 30 minutes.

4. Add salt and pepper to taste.

5. Add the ham, cream, and butter and continue cooking, uncovered, until heated through, about 10 more minutes.

MAKES 8 TO 10 SERVINGS

1 pound split peas
6 cups chicken stock
6 cups water
1 teaspoon dried thyme
4 bay leaves
2 cups peeled and diced yellow onion (from about 1 large onion)
2 cups peeled and diced carrot (from about 4 large carrots)
1 cup chopped celery (from about 4 stalks)
2 tablespoons extra-virgin olive oil
2 tablespoons fresh minced garlic
2 pounds Yukon Gold potatoes, diced (from 4 to 5 large potatoes)
Table salt and freshly ground black pepper
1½ pounds ham, diced
½ cup heavy cream
¼ cup butter

RED LEAF LETTUCE SALAD WITH RASPBERRY-CITRUS VINAIGRETTE & SUGARED ALMONDS

•}}}❖{{{• •}}}❖{{{• •}}}❖{{{•

My mom was in charge of writing the monthly newsletter for the ladies auxiliary at church when I was growing up. Even though I'm fairly certain we had a home computer and dot matrix printer, she always designed the newsletters by hand. She wrote everything out in her lovely handwriting and drew little pictures on the borders and around the title. My first encounter with this colorful salad recipe was in one of those beautiful newsletters, so it has always seemed elegant and extra special to me. The bright, fresh flavors are a nice contrast to the hearty soup we eat on Christmas Eve.

MAKES 8 TO 10 SERVINGS

For the sugared almonds:
¾ cup slivered almonds
3 tablespoons sugar
Pinch of table salt

....

2 large heads red leaf lettuce
3 to 4 medium apples, peeled, cored, and julienned (see facing page)
4 large sweet oranges, peeled and sectioned
1 small red onion, very thinly sliced

1. To make the sugared almonds, in a small sauté pan over medium heat, combine the almonds, sugar, and salt. Stir gently until the sugar is melted and almonds are golden, 5 to 10 minutes. Pour the candied almonds onto a piece of aluminum foil to cool. Once they are cool and dry, break the almonds apart and set aside.

2. Remove the lettuce cores, tear the leaves into bite-size pieces, and put them in a large serving bowl. Add the apples, oranges, and red onion; set aside.

3. To make the vinaigrette, in a blender or in the bowl of a food processor, blend the oil, orange juice, sugar, raspberry vinegar, oregano, parsley, garlic, mustard, salt, and pepper until the herbs and garlic are finely chopped and the mixture looks mostly uniform, about 30 seconds. Pour it over the salad, toss, top with the sugared almonds, and serve.

To julienne the apples, start by cutting the peeled, cored apple in half, just like you would if you wanted to eat it for an afternoon snack. Cut each half into thin slices, about ⅛ inch thick, then cut each thin slice into sticks.

Winter is the perfect time of year to make this salad because of the wide variety of citrus fruits available at local grocery stores. My family loves Cara Cara oranges, which have beautiful pinkish-red flesh and a super-sweet flavor. Feel free to experiment with other sweet citrus fruits like tangerines and mandarins.

If you don't have a blender or food processor, you can still make this delicious vinaigrette dressing. Finely mince the oregano, parsley, and garlic and, in a container with a tight-fitting lid such as a 16-ounce mason jar, combine all vinaigrette ingredients. Make sure the lid is securely on the container, then shake vigorously until the dressing is well mixed.

For the vinaigrette:
½ cup extra-virgin olive oil
⅓ cup freshly squeezed orange juice (from about 1 to 2 medium oranges)
3 tablespoons sugar
3 tablespoons raspberry vinegar
2 tablespoons coarsely chopped fresh oregano, or 2 teaspoons dried oregano leaves
1 tablespoon coarsely chopped fresh parsley, or 1 teaspoon dried parsley
1 clove garlic
1 teaspoon Dijon mustard
½ teaspoon table salt
Freshly ground black pepper

Special equipment:
Blender or food processor

NANA'S SAVORY MULTIGRAIN HERB BREAD

•})}•⚙•{{{• •})}•⚙•{{{• •})}•⚙•{{{•

Every Christmas, my nana makes her special herb bread. She bakes it in big soup cans, so the loaves turn out perfectly round and uniquely ridged. She got the recipe from a magazine back in the 1960s and has been making it every Christmas for the past fifty-something years. I have photocopies of her originals with five decades of notes and changes scrawled in the margins in her handwriting. This bread is delicious fresh, and even better toasted and slathered in butter. It's the perfect partner for a big bowl of Scandinavian split pea soup.

MAKES 2 LOAVES

1 cup old-fashioned
rolled oats
2 cups boiling water
⅓ cup warm water
1 tablespoon active
dry yeast
Pinch of sugar
⅓ cup honey
3 tablespoons butter
2 teaspoons table salt
2 teaspoons dried
summer savory
1 teaspoon dried basil
½ teaspoon dried parsley
½ teaspoon anise seed
¼ teaspoon dried thyme
⅓ cup wheat germ or
multigrain hot cereal
6 cups flour

1. In a large bowl with a wooden spoon or in the bowl of a stand mixer fitted with the dough hook attachment, add the oats and pour the boiling water over them. Allow to sit for 30 minutes.

2. In a small bowl or glass measuring cup, combine the warm water, yeast, and sugar, and set aside for 5 minutes to allow the yeast to activate. The mixture should grow and be bubbly (see page xix for tips on making yeast breads).

3. Pour the yeast mixture into the oats. Add the honey, butter, salt, and herbs and mix just until combined.

4. Add the wheat germ and 4 cups of the flour. Mix until combined. Continue adding the flour ¼ cup at a time until the dough is no longer sticky when you lightly touch it. You will probably not use all 6 cups of the flour.

5. Put the dough on a well-floured counter, and knead by hand for another 2 or 3 minutes, until the dough is smooth and elastic.

6. Lightly spray the mixing bowl with nonstick cooking spray (no need to wash it first), put the dough in the bowl, cover with plastic wrap, and allow the dough to rise in a warm spot until doubled in size, 45 minutes to 1 hour.

CONTINUED

7. Punch down the dough, knead it for another minute, and divide it into two equal portions. Spray two 9-by-5-inch loaf pans with nonstick cooking spray, shape each portion of dough into a log, and place the dough in the prepared pans.

8. Cover the pans with plastic wrap and allow the dough to rise for another 30 minutes.

9. Preheat the oven to 350 degrees F. Bake the herb bread for 30 to 35 minutes, until the top of each loaf is golden and it sounds hollow when tapped. If you have a probe thermometer, you can measure the internal temperature of the loaves. They should be 190 degrees F.

10. Immediately turn the loaves out onto a cooling rack to cool. Rub the tops with butter while they're still warm.

VARIATIONS:

• Instead of the summer savory, basil, parsley, anise seed, and thyme herb blend called for in the recipe, you can use 2 teaspoons dried, crumbled sage leaves (make sure to pick out any sticks or bits of stem); 1 teaspoon dried marjoram leaves; and 1 teaspoon caraway seeds.

• If you happen to have sourdough starter in your refrigerator, you are probably always looking for ways to use it! This bread is a great recipe for incorporating a little sourdough. Simply stir in ⅓ cup sourdough starter when you add the wheat germ. You'll end up adding a little more flour overall than if you didn't add sourdough starter, but you won't use much more than the 6 cups flour listed in the recipe.

RASPBERRY PUDDING WITH CREAM
(DANISH RØDGRØD MED FLØD)

•}})❁{{(• •}})❁{{(• •}})❁{{(•

The highlight of Christmas Eve dinner at Nana's house is always the raspberry pudding served with cream. When my grandparents moved back to the United States after living in Sweden for a few years, they brought lots of new traditions with them, and this is one of the family's favorites. *Rødgrød med fløt* is traditionally a Danish summer treat because of the abundance of fresh berries in the area, but thanks to frozen berries, you can make it all year. I always top mine with a generous serving of cream, and I usually add another splash of cream halfway through! In my opinion it's best eaten out of a beautiful crystal dish with a tiny, ornate spoon, the way Nana serves it every year.

1. In a medium saucepan over medium heat, heat the raspberries and 3 cups of the water until the fruit is soft and breaks apart, about 25 minutes.

2. Puree the fruit mixture. My favorite way to do this is with a stick or immersion blender, but a regular blender or food mill will also work. A food processor will work as well, but you will have to work in batches. Strain the mixture through a fine mesh sieve to remove all seeds. Pour the strained fruit juice into a clean medium saucepan.

3. Add the sugar and cook the mixture over medium heat until the sugar is dissolved, about 2 minutes.

4. In a glass measuring cup or small bowl, combine the cornstarch with the remaining ½ cup water. Whisk until combined. Add the cornstarch mixture to the fruit juice mixture, whisking constantly. Continue whisking while bringing the mixture to a boil. Cook until thickened, about 5 minutes.

5. Pour into small bowls or parfait dishes. Cover each dish with a small piece of plastic wrap, and put the plastic wrap directly on the surface of the pudding to prevent a skin from forming while the pudding cools. Refrigerate until set, at least 3 hours. Serve with the heavy cream.

MAKES 10 TO 12 SERVINGS

1½ cups fresh or frozen raspberries
3 ½ cups cold water, divided
1 cup sugar
¼ cup cornstarch
Heavy cream, for serving

Special equipment:
Blender, food mill, or food processor
Fine mesh sieve

TANTE KARI'S HOT ALMOND-CITRUS PUNCH

•)))◆(((• •)))◆(((• •)))◆(((•

My mom's oldest sister, Kari, started making this holiday punch before I can even remember, and it has become a longtime Christmas staple in my family. The combination of orange and almond flavors is classically Scandinavian. It's the kind of beverage you'll want to sip while basking in the soft glow of Christmas tree lights.

**MAKES ABOUT
5½ QUARTS**

15 cups water

6 cups bottled orange juice (not from concentrate)

3 cups sugar

¾ cup freshly squeezed lemon juice (from about 3 medium lemons)

4 teaspoons almond extract

2 teaspoons vanilla extract

Orange slices, for garnish

1. In a large pot over medium heat, mix all the ingredients except the orange slices. Heat the punch until steaming. Serve hot, and garnish with the orange slices.

VARIATION

• Add ½ shot of dark spiced rum to 1 cup of hot punch for an extra kick.

Candles play a huge role in the Christmas season all across Scandinavia. Every Sunday for the four weeks before Christmas, people light Advent candles in their homes. Lucia Day features candles prominently in Lucia's flaming crown, and people both participating in and watching the Lucia procession hold candles. Houses have electric candles in each window. And Swedish angel chimes use the heat from candles to power tiny gold windmills that make a soft, tinkling sound as they spin. All of these candles help keep the darkness of the Scandinavian winter at bay.

HAND-STAMPED WRAPPING PAPER

•})}⊕{{{• •})}⊕{{{• •})}⊕{{{•

I love the simplicity of Scandinavian style, especially when it comes to Christmas decorations. A minimalist color palette of red and white, complemented by natural shades of evergreen boughs and golden wheat, and simple motifs like hearts, stars, snowflakes, and trees, creates an atmosphere that is clean, rustic, and peaceful. This easy hand-stamped wrapping paper gives presents a special touch of Nordic charm.

1. Turn to the wrapping paper template. Lay the paper on top of the template, and trace the chosen design with a pencil.

2. Place the traced design facedown on top of the craft foam sheet, and rub the back all over with your fingernail or with the pencil to transfer the pencil marks from the paper to the foam. Before picking up the paper, gently lift a corner of it to make sure the entire design has been transferred.

3. Cut your design out of foam with the scissors. Lay out each foam piece on top of a small wooden block. Carefully peel the backing off each foam piece, stick it onto the wood, and press firmly.

4. Roll out a few feet of wrapping paper, and place some heavy objects on the corners to prevent the paper from rolling back up.

5. Squirt some red, white, or green paint onto a piece of cardboard. Use the paintbrush to apply a thin layer of paint to the foam stamp. This might seem like an extra step, but it keeps your stamp and wrapping paper cleaner and produces a much nicer result. Firmly press the stamp onto the wrapping paper and carefully lift it straight back up. You can use the stamp two or three times before reapplying paint.

MATERIALS & TOOLS:

Hand-Stamped Wrapping Paper template (page 224)

Plain white paper

Pencil

Adhesive-backed craft foam

Sharp scissors

2-inch wooden blocks, for mounting stamps

Rolls of blank wrapping paper in either white or kraft

Craft paint in shades of red, white, and green (see page 209 for exact colors)

Paper plate, cardboard, or something to put the paint on

Small paintbrush or sponge brush

CONTINUED

step 1

6. Repeat step 5 as many times as desired. When finished, immediately wash your paintbrush and stamp with cool water to remove any excess paint. Allow them to air-dry.

7. Once the stamped wrapping paper has dried completely, then use it as you would regular wrapping paper.

step 2

Angel chimes are a Swedish Christmas staple in my family. Angel chimes feature a small gold tower topped with a little windmill that spins horizontally. Attached to the windmill are tiny angels that fly around in circles, bumping against little bells as they spin, making a delicate chiming sound as they go. The whole thing is powered by the heat from little candles attached to the base of the tower.

step 3

WHEAT WREATHS

Scandinavian holiday decorations are simple and rustic, often made of straw and wheat. Place one of these handmade wheat wreaths on your front door as a beautiful Nordic way to welcome visitors to your house during the holiday season.

1. Lay the inside ring of an embroidery hoop on a flat work surface. You won't use the outside of the ring. Use the scissors to cut 36 inches of the red grosgrain ribbon. Fold the ribbon in half, put the folded end through the middle of the embroidery hoop from front to back, bring the two loose ends of the ribbon over the hoop and through the looped ribbon end, and pull to tighten.

2. Take three stalks of wheat in a small bundle. Trim the ends so that they are just 3 inches longer than the head of the stalk. Position the bundle of wheat on the embroidery hoop so that the wheat goes straight across the red ribbon at the top of the circle, with the heads of the wheat stalks on the right. Give the bundle a little twist counterclockwise until the outermost wheat stalk extends off the embroidery hoop slightly. Hot glue the bundle of wheat in place.

3. Trim another bundle of three stalks to the same length as before. Position them on the embroidery hoop at a similar angle as the first bunch, but move them about 2 inches farther around the circle counterclockwise.

4. Repeat with more wheat stalks until the entire embroidery hoop is covered in wheat. As you get close to the original bundle of wheat stalks, make sure you tuck the ends of the new bundles under the heads of the first wheat bundle so that they are hidden.

MATERIALS & TOOLS:

Circular embroidery
  hoops in various sizes
1-inch-wide red
  grosgrain ribbon
Scissors
3 bunches wheat stalks
Hot glue gun
Hot glue sticks

> **HOW TO SAY *MERRY CHRISTMAS* IN SCANDINAVIA:**
>
> Norway: *Gledelig Jul*
>
> Sweden: *God Jul*
>
> Denmark: *Glaedelig Jul*
>
> Finland: *Hyvää Joulua*

CONTINUED

5. To make a half-circle wreath, place the first bundle of wheat one-quarter of the way around the circle from the red ribbon hanger. Glue bundles of wheat until you get to the bottom of the wreath. Glue another bundle of wheat on the opposite side of the embroidery hoop from the first bundle, pointing in the opposite direction. Glue bundles of wheat until you get to the bottom of the wreath and meet the bundles from the other side. Glue a few extra heads of wheat in place to cover any visible hot glue or to cover the spot where the two bundles of wheat meet in the middle.

6. To make a quarter-circle wreath, follow the directions in step 5, but only glue wheat bundles on a quarter of the circle.

7. Hang your wreaths from a door or window, or on the wall.

You can find bunches of wheat stalks in the floral department of most large craft stores.

Save the trimmed stalks to make Straw Star Ornaments (page 177).

STRAW STAR ORNAMENTS

•⟩⟩⟩•❂•⟨⟨⟨•⟩⟩⟩•❂•⟨⟨⟨•⟩⟩⟩•❂•⟨⟨⟨•

Nana and Poppy take great pride in dressing every corner of their house to the nines for Christmas, especially their Christmas tree. My grandparents' Christmas tree is always draped with Norwegian and Swedish flags, little wooden Viking ships, and dozens and dozens of traditional Scandinavian straw ornaments. Stars, hearts, and little *tomten* or *nisser* made of straw or raffia are common sights on Nordic Christmas trees. They look sweet and old-fashioned nestled in among the soft white lights and green pine boughs.

1. Use the ruler and scissors to trim five pieces of straw to a length of 3 inches each. Lay them out on a flat work surface so that they overlap to make a star. Allow the pieces of straw to form small Xs at the points of the stars. Use the hot glue at each star point where two pieces of straw cross each other. Allow the glue to dry completely.

2. Cut a piece of red embroidery floss that is 12 inches long. Wrap the embroidery floss around the junction five times, leaving about 2 inches of floss free. Use the two loose ends to tie a secure knot; trim any extra floss. Repeat with the other four points of the star.

3. Cut an 8-inch length of embroidery floss. Tuck one end of the floss through one of the points of the star, bring the ends together, and knot them together to make a loop.

MATERIALS & TOOLS:

Ruler

Scissors

Straw

Hot glue gun

Hot glue sticks

Single-strand pearl cotton embroidery floss in red

If you make the wheat wreath on page 173, be sure to save the trimmed stalks. The narrower ends are perfect for this project.

Single-strand embroidery floss is right next to the little skeins of thicker, multi-strand embroidery floss at craft or sewing stores. Instead of being packaged in a long, twisted bundle, it comes wound in a ball and is very easy to work with.

Birthday Treats

THE HIGHLIGHT OF ANY BIRTHDAY is the cake. Scandinavians tend to keep their cakes a little less loaded with frosting than we do in America. They prefer theirs with a drizzle of sauce, a sprinkling of confectioners' or pearl sugar, or a cloud of whipped cream. This chapter is a collection of traditional and Scandinavian-inspired cakes to make every birthday celebration memorable.

CREATING THE GATHERING

Birthday gatherings should be fun and colorful! Scandinavians decorate for every holiday with their national flag, and that includes birthdays. If you have a Paper Flag Garland (page 110) or flag toothpicks, be sure to use them. Get in-season flower arrangements and place them on the food table, on your porch, and in any other spot you want to look festive and welcoming. You can have one cake at your birthday gathering, or all four cakes from this chapter!

RECIPES

Cream Cake with Fresh Strawberries (Norwegian Bløtkake)
Spiced Pear Bundt Cake with Homemade Caramel Sauce
Chocolate Sticky Cake (Swedish Kladdkaka)
Caramel Almond Sponge Cake (Swedish Toscakake)

PROJECTS

Dipped Beeswax Birthday Candles
Birthday Flag Banner
Felt Birthday Crowns

CREAM CAKE WITH FRESH STRAWBERRIES (NORWEGIAN BLØTKAKE)

•})}⦿{{{• •})}⦿{{{• •})}⦿{{{•

Bløtkake, with its layers of vanilla sponge cake, fresh berries, and piles of whipped cream, is the Scandinavian version of strawberry shortcake. It is a Norwegian birthday favorite, beloved by people of all ages, and is what my family always eats for dessert on Syttende Mai (Norway's national holiday) and Midsummer.

MAKES 10 TO 12 SERVINGS

1¼ cups sugar
½ cup butter
1½ teaspoons vanilla extract
3 eggs
2 cups flour
2 teaspoons baking powder
½ teaspoon table salt
1 cup buttermilk

For the filling and topping:
1½ pounds fresh strawberries
1 tablespoon granulated sugar
1 pint whipping cream
¾ cup confectioners' sugar
1½ teaspoons vanilla extract

Special equipment:
2 (8-inch) round cake pans

1. Preheat the oven to 350 degrees F. Butter and flour the bottom and sides of two 8-inch round cake pans, shaking out any excess flour.

2. In a large mixing bowl with an electric mixer or in the bowl of a stand mixer fitted with the paddle attachment, beat the sugar and butter on medium speed until light and fluffy, about 1 minute. Add the vanilla and 1 egg, and beat until smooth, then add the remaining eggs one at a time, beating between each addition. Scrape down the sides of the bowl with a spatula as needed.

3. In a small bowl, combine the flour, baking powder, and salt; set aside.

4. With the mixer on low, add one-third of the flour mixture, then half of the buttermilk, beating each addition just until combined. Repeat until all of the cake ingredients have been added. Turn the mixer to high speed and beat 30 seconds more.

5. Divide the batter evenly between the prepared cake pans. Bake for 20 to 23 minutes, until a toothpick inserted in the center of each cake comes out clean.

CONTINUED

6. While the cakes are baking, make the filling and topping. Finely chop the berries (reserving a few whole berries for garnishing the finished cake), then put them in a bowl with the granulated sugar, and refrigerate until you are ready to assemble the cake. To make the topping, in a medium bowl, whip the cream until stiff peaks form. Add the confectioners' sugar and vanilla, beating until combined.

7. Remove the cakes from the oven. Allow them to cool for 10 minutes in the pans. While the cakes are cooling, lightly spray a cooling rack with nonstick cooking spray, then flip the cakes out onto the cooling rack and allow them to cool completely.

8. To assemble the cream cake, place one 8-inch cake on a serving plate flat side up. Top with half of the berries and half of any juice that has accumulated in the bowl, then half of the whipped cream. Repeat with the remaining cake layer, berries, and whipped cream. Refrigerate the cake for several hours before serving to allow the berry juice to soak into the cake layers. Garnish with fresh, whole strawberries before serving.

HOW TO SAY *HAPPY BIRTHDAY* IN SCANDINAVIA:

Norway: *Gratulerer med dagen*

Sweden: *Grattis på födelsedagen*

Denmark: *Tillykke med fødselsdagen*

Finland: *Hyvää syntymäpäivää*

SPICED PEAR BUNDT CAKE WITH HOMEMADE CARAMEL SAUCE

•⫸✦⫷• •⫸✦⫷• •⫸✦⫷•

This spicy pear cake, with hints of cinnamon, nutmeg, cardamom, and cloves, is perfect for crisp autumn evenings and cozy winter gatherings. Thanks to its beautiful shape and delicate crumb, it is elegant without being fussy; it needs no more adornment than a drizzle of buttery, homemade caramel sauce and a dollop of sweet whipped cream.

1. Preheat the oven to 350 degrees F. If using a dark Bundt pan, preheat the oven to 325 degrees F. Generously butter and flour the interior of the Bundt pan, shaking out any excess flour.

2. In a large bowl with an electric mixer or in the bowl of a stand mixer fitted with the paddle attachment, combine the sugars and butter. Beat on medium speed until fluffy, about 1 minute. Add the vanilla and the eggs one at a time, beating on medium speed after each addition until smooth.

3. In a medium bowl, combine the flour, baking powder, baking soda, salt, and spices.

4. With the mixer on low speed, add one-third of the flour mixture to the butter-and-sugar mixture, followed by half of the milk. Continue alternating flour and milk until all have been added. Scrape down the sides and bottom of the bowl with a spatula, then beat the batter on high speed for 20 to 30 seconds.

5. Pour half of the batter into the pan. Sprinkle half of the pears evenly over the top of the batter. Pour the rest of the batter into the pan, and cover with the remaining pears. Bake the cake for 65 minutes, or until the cake begins to pull away from the edges of the pan, and a bamboo skewer inserted in the center of the cake comes out clean.

CONTINUED

MAKES 12 TO 16 SERVINGS

1 cup granulated sugar
¾ cup lightly packed light brown sugar
¾ cup butter, softened
2 teaspoons vanilla extract
4 eggs, at room temperature
3 cups flour
1 teaspoon baking powder
½ teaspoon baking soda
½ teaspoon table salt
1 teaspoon ground cinnamon
½ teaspoon ground nutmeg
¼ teaspoon ground cardamom
⅛ teaspoon ground cloves
1½ cups whole milk
3 cups peeled, chopped, and diced soft, ripe pears (from about 4 pears)
Lightly sweetened whipped cream, for serving

6. Allow the cake to cool in the pan for 10 minutes, then gently invert it onto a cooling rack to cool completely.

7. While the cake bakes and cools, make the caramel. In a small, heavy-bottomed saucepan with tall sides over medium heat, cook the sugar and water until the sugar dissolves, 4 to 5 minutes. Increase the heat to high and cook until the mixture caramelizes and turns amber-colored, about 7 minutes. It should be the color of clover honey.

8. Immediately remove the caramel from the heat, and add the cream, whisking constantly. The mixture will sputter and splash, so wearing long sleeves and/or an oven mitt is a great idea. If the mixture seizes up, whisk it over medium heat just until it becomes smooth.

9. Add the butter and vanilla, whisk until smooth, and allow it to cool to room temperature.

10. Serve the cake at room temperature. Drizzle slices with caramel and top with the whipped cream.

For the caramel:
¾ cup sugar
½ cup water
½ cup plus 2 tablespoons
   heavy cream
¼ cup butter
1 teaspoon vanilla extract

Special equipment:
Bundt pan

CHOCOLATE STICKY CAKE (SWEDISH KLADDKAKA)

•}}}•❂•{{{• •}}}•❂•{{{• •}}}•❂•{{{•

When we think of Scandinavian desserts, we usually think of butter and sugar and
almonds and spices—anything but chocolate. But this easy Swedish cake is a chocolate
lover's dream come true! It is so simple to make that even kids can help out, and it bakes
up crisp on the edges and gooey in the center, like brownies. You'll become a fan after
the first fudgy bite!

MAKES 8 SERVINGS

1 cup granulated sugar
2 eggs
1 teaspoon vanilla extract
½ teaspoon table salt
¼ cup cocoa powder
¾ cup flour
½ cup plus 2 tablespoons
   butter, melted
Confectioners' sugar,
   for serving (optional)
Lightly sweetened
   whipped cream or
   ice cream, for serving
   (optional)

Special equipment:
8-inch round cake pan

1. Preheat the oven to 350 degrees F. Butter an 8-inch round
cake pan and dust the inside with either flour or cocoa powder,
shaking out the excess.

2. In a medium bowl, combine the sugar, eggs, vanilla, and salt
with a whisk until smooth.

3. In a small bowl, combine the cocoa powder and flour, then
whisk the dry ingredients into the sugar mixture until smooth.

4. Gently whisk in the melted butter.

5. Bake for 20 to 25 minutes, until the edges of the cake start to
pull away from the pan and the top looks set.

6. Let the cake cool in the pan for 3 to 5 minutes, then flip it
onto a large dinner plate, then immediately flip it again onto
your serving plate so that it is right side up.

7. Serve warm, dusted with the confectioners' sugar, and/or
topped with whipped cream or ice cream. Store at room temperature, covered. Leftovers can be reheated in the microwave
for about 15 seconds.

CARAMEL ALMOND SPONGE CAKE (SWEDISH TOSCAKAKE)

•}}}◉{{{• •}}}◉{{{• •}}}◉{{{•

My friend Maria Stordahl Nelson, who writes the charming blog *Pink Patisserie*, is three-fourths Scandinavian. She grew up in the Ballard neighborhood in Seattle, Washington, taking part in all of the Scandinavian cultural opportunities in the area. She marched in parades in her *bunad*, ate treats from the Danish bakery, and learned how to make all of her family's traditional Norwegian and Swedish recipes—including this delicious *toscakake*, a buttery yellow sponge cake topped with a stick-to-your-teeth caramel and an almond layer. In Maria's family they sometimes make a double batch of the caramel topping because it's just that amazing. After your first bite of *toscakake*, you'll undoubtedly agree!

1. Preheat the oven to 350 degrees F. Butter and flour an 8-inch springform pan, shaking out any excess flour.

2. In a large bowl with an electric mixer or in the bowl of a stand mixer fitted with the paddle attachment, beat the eggs and sugar on medium speed until light and lemon colored, about 30 seconds. With the mixer on low, slowly add the melted butter and cream, and beat until combined.

3. In a small bowl, combine the flour and baking powder. With the mixer on low, add the flour mixture to the egg mixture. Beat on medium speed until smooth, scraping down the sides of the bowl as necessary.

4. Pour the batter into the springform pan, and bake for 20 to 25 minutes, until the top is golden and the cake is set.

5. While the cake is baking, make the caramel topping. In a small saucepan over medium heat, whisk together the brown sugar, butter, flour, and cream until the butter is melted and the mixture is syrupy. Stir in the almonds and remove the saucepan from the heat.

CONTINUED

MAKES 8 TO 12 SERVINGS

½ cup butter, melted
¾ cup flour
2 eggs
⅔ cup sugar
¼ cup heavy cream
1 teaspoon baking powder

For the caramel topping:
½ cup lightly packed light brown sugar
½ cup butter
2 tablespoons flour
2 tablespoons heavy cream
1 cup sliced almonds
Lightly sweetened whipped cream, for serving

Special equipment:
8-inch springform pan

6. When the cake is done, spread the caramel topping evenly over the cake, and bake for another 5 minutes, until the entire surface is light and bubbly.

7. Remove the pan from the oven and allow the cake to cool for 5 minutes before running a butter knife around the inside edge and removing the sides of the pan.

8. Serve warm or at room temperature, topped with the whipped cream.

If you don't have a springform pan, you can use a standard 8-inch round cake pan instead. Be sure to serve the cake straight from the pan; do not try to remove it first.

There's a very famous Scandinavian cake that is notably absent from this chapter: the sandwich cake or *smörgåstårta*. They are popular in Sweden and Finland, and they are actually savory cakes made of sandwich ingredients. Layers of bread filled with ham, cucumbers, shrimp salad, hard-boiled eggs, radishes, carrot strips, and more, all piled high, frosted with savory cream cheese spreads, and decorated with salmon rosettes, cherry tomatoes, olives, and more veggies. And don't forget the flag toothpicks! Making this is as simple as layering all the ingredients—just don't forget to tell your guests what kind of cake it is!

DIPPED BEESWAX BIRTHDAY CANDLES

·⟩⟩⟩✦⟨⟨⟨·⟩⟩⟩✦⟨⟨⟨·⟩⟩⟩✦⟨⟨⟨·

These candles feel both down-to-earth and elegant. I love the warm, subtle spiciness of beeswax's fragrance and its beautiful golden color. Topping a from-scratch birthday cake with tiny, homemade beeswax candles makes the occasion even more special.

1. Preheat the oven to 175 degrees F. Place the filtered beeswax in the can, and place the can in the oven until the beeswax is completely melted. You need about 5 inches of melted beeswax. Add more as beeswax as necessary.

2. For each pair of candles you want to make, use the scissors to cut 14 inches of wicking.

3. Securely tie a nut or washer to each end of the wicking. This will help weigh down the wick before the candles are heavy enough to weigh themselves down.

4. Lay the broomstick or dowel across the gap between two countertops or kitchen chairs. Cover the floor underneath with newspaper, paper towels, or garbage bags.

5. Holding the wicking in the very center with both ends hanging down, dip both ends of the wicking into the melted beeswax to a depth of about 4 inches. Your motions should be smooth and unhurried. Pull the wicking back up, drape it across the prepared broomstick, and allow it to drip and cool. While you wait, you can dip more pairs!

CONTINUED

MATERIALS & TOOLS:

Filtered beeswax

Clean can at least
8 inches tall

Square braid wicking,
size #5/10

Scissors

Hardware nuts

Broomstick or long,
thick dowel

Newspaper, paper towels,
or garbage bags

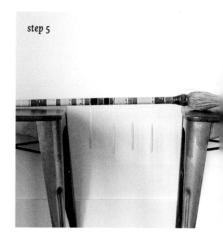

step 5

6. Once the first pair of candles is cool enough to touch, straighten out any crookedness in the wicking, and dip again, just as before. You can straighten the candles after they have cooled slightly each time by gently rolling them on a clean counter or work surface.

7. When the candles have enough beeswax on them to weigh them down (after four or five dips), cut the nuts off the bottom and continue dipping.

8. Repeat the dipping and cooling steps with all pairs of candles until they are about as big around as a pencil.

9. After dipping the candles for the last time, hang the candles and allow them to cool completely. Cut the cooled candles apart and trim the wicks.

You can easily make larger beeswax tapers following these same directions. You'll just need to adjust the size of can, the amount of beeswax, and the length of wicking you use.

BIRTHDAY FLAG BANNER

·))·◉·((·· ·))·◉·((·· ·))·◉·((··

One of the main decorations for a Scandinavian birthday is the national flag, which serves as inspiration for this sweet and simple birthday banner. Hung on the wall above the birthday table, it makes a darling addition to the party décor, especially when paired with paper chains, lengths of pom-pom trim, and simple garlands made of punched paper circles glued onto striped baker's twine.

FOR THE NORWEGIAN BANNER:

1. Trace the birthday flag template with a pencil onto a piece of plain white paper, and use the scissors to cut it out. Trace the flag shape nine times onto the red patterned card stock and seven times onto the blue patterned card stock. Cut out the flags.

2. Cut two strips of white card stock that measure 1 by 4 inches and two strips that measure 1 by 6 inches. Out of the leftover blue paper, cut two strips that measure ½ by 4 inches and two strips that measure ½ by 6 inches. Glue each of the shorter white strips across the center of a red flag, then glue each of the longer white strips in the opposite direction across the center of the same red flags. Repeat with the blue strips. Use the scissors to trim the white and blue paper that hangs off the notched end of the flag. These two pieces of card stock should now resemble Norwegian flags.

3. Lay out all of the plain red and blue paper flags in two rows, alternating colors. Begin and end the top row with blue flags, and include five flags in this row. Begin and end the bottom row with red flags, and include nine flags in this row.

4. Spell *HAPPY* on the top row of flags using white letters, and spell *BIRTHDAY!* on the bottom row of flags. Affix each letter to the corresponding paper flag. If using chipboard letters, attach them with glue or double-sided tape.

MATERIALS & TOOLS:

Birthday Flag Banner template (page 225)

Pencil

Plain white paper

Scissors

12-by-12-inch patterned card stock or heavy scrapbooking paper in the colors of the national flags

- **NORWAY:** 2 sheets each of red and navy blue, 1 sheet of white

- **SWEDEN:** 2 sheets each of sky blue and sunshine yellow

- **DENMARK:** 2 different patterns of red (2 sheets each) and 1 sheet of white

- **FINLAND:** 2 different patterns of royal blue (2 sheets each) and 1 sheet of white

Glue stick or double-sided tape

CONTINUED

White adhesive or chipboard letters spelling *HAPPY BIRTHDAY!*

Single-hole paper punch

2 lengths of thick cotton twine, one 58 inches and the other 68 inches long

Norwegian Banner

Swedish Banner

5. Using a hole punch, punch a hole in each of the top corners of each flag. Be sure to punch holes in the flags from step 2 as well. Place a national flag at the beginning and end of the *HAPPY* row of flags.

6. Thread the paper flags onto the twine in order so that the twine runs behind each flag. The *HAPPY* row goes on the 58-inch length of twine, and the *BIRTHDAY!* row goes on the 68-inch length of twine. Leave some space between each flag, and leave 12 inches of twine on each end.

FOR THE SWEDISH BANNER:

1. Trace the birthday flag template with a pencil onto a piece of plain white paper, and use the scissors to cut it out. Then trace the flag shape nine times onto the sky-blue patterned card stock and seven times onto the sunshine-yellow patterned card stock. Cut out the flags.

2. Out of the leftover yellow paper, cut two strips that measure 1 by 4 inches and two strips that measure 1 by 6 inches. Glue each of the shorter yellow strips across the center of a blue flag, then glue each of the longer yellow strips in the opposite direction across the center of the same blue flags. Use the scissors to trim the yellow paper that hangs off the notched end of the flag. These two pieces of card stock should now resemble Swedish flags.

3. Lay out all of the plain yellow and blue paper flags in two rows, alternating colors. Begin and end the top row with yellow flags, and include five flags in this row. Begin and end the bottom row with blue flags, and include nine flags in this row.

4. Follow steps 4 to 6 from the directions for the Norwegian banner.

FOR THE DANISH BANNER:

1. Trace the birthday flag template with a pencil onto a piece of plain white paper, and use the scissors to cut it out. Designate one style of red paper as pattern A, and the other as pattern B. Trace the flag shape nine times onto pattern A card stock and seven times onto pattern B card stock. Cut out the flags.

2. Cut two strips of white card stock that measure 1 by 4 inches and two strips that measure 1 by 6 inches. Glue each of the shorter white strips across the center of a pattern A flag, then glue each of the longer white strips in the opposite direction across the center of the same red flags. Use the scissors to trim the white paper that hangs off the notched end of the flag. These two pieces of card stock should now resemble Danish flags and should be identical to each other.

3. Lay out all of the plain red flags in two rows, alternating patterns. Begin and end the top row with pattern B flags, and include five flags in this row. Begin and end the bottom row with pattern A flags, and include nine flags in this row.

4. Follow steps 4 to 6 from the directions for the Norwegian banner.

FOR THE FINNISH BANNER:

1. Trace the birthday flag template with a pencil onto a piece of plain white paper, and use the scissors to cut it out. Designate one style of blue paper as pattern A, and the other as pattern B. Trace the flag shape seven times onto pattern A card stock and seven times onto pattern B card stock. Trace the flag shape two times onto the white card stock. Cut out the flags.

2. Cut two strips of blue card stock that measure 1 by 4 inches and two strips that measure 1 by 6 inches. It doesn't matter which pattern of paper you use, but all of the strips need to be

CONTINUED

Danish Banner

Finnish Banner

cut from the same pattern. Glue each of the shorter blue strips across the center of a white flag, then glue each of the longer blue strips in the opposite direction across the center of the white flags. Use the scissors to trim the blue paper that hangs off the notched end of the flag. These two pieces of card stock should now resemble Finnish flags and should be identical to each other.

3. Lay out all of the plain blue flags in two rows, alternating patterns. Begin and end the top row with pattern A flags, and include five flags in this row. Begin and end the bottom row with pattern B flags, and include nine flags in this row.

4. Follow steps 4 to 6 from the directions for the Norwegian banner.

To hang the banners, I used a piece of ⅛-inch-thick cotton twine from the rope section of the hardware store. It comes prepackaged in more than enough length.

If you can't find 12-by-12-inch pieces of card stock or heavy scrapbooking paper in the colors or patterns you want, you can use 8½-by-11-inch sheets instead. Just buy one extra piece in each color or pattern.

FELT BIRTHDAY CROWNS

When my second daughter was very little, a dear friend made her a fabric crown for her birthday, and she's loved wearing it on her special day every year since. These felt crowns can be carefully folded away after each birthday celebration and saved until the next year. The ribbons that are used to tie them on are fully adjustable, so they fit birthday boys and girls of all ages. The felt crowns are inspired by the crowns pictured in the coats of arms of all three Scandinavian countries and Finland, and the gorgeous crowns of the Scandinavian monarchies.

MATERIALS & TOOLS:

1 (12-by-18-inch) sheet wool-blend felt (see page 209 for exact colors)

Sharp scissors

Heavy-duty double-sided fusible interfacing

Ironing board

Iron

Clean kitchen towel or pressing cloth

Pencil

Ruler

Single-hole paper punch

Ribbon in a contrasting color

1. Cut the sheet of felt in half with the scissors so that you have two pieces that are 6 by 18 inches. Cut a piece of fusible interfacing to 6 by 18 inches as well.

2. Lay out one piece of felt on the ironing board. Lay the fusible interfacing on top of the felt with the bumpy side down and the paper side up. Iron the interfacing onto the felt following the directions on the interfacing packaging, and allow the felt to cool completely.

3. Peel the paper off the cooled felt/interfacing combo. Place the other piece of felt on top of the interfacing, cover it with a clean kitchen towel or pressing cloth, and press down firmly while ironing to adhere the two pieces of felt to each other. Allow the felt to cool completely.

4. Lay out the cooled felt so that it is wider than it is tall. Next, make an outline of dots to create the points of the crown. Make a small dot with the pencil along the top edge 1½ inches in from the left edge. From that dot, make a series of dots every 3 inches. You will make six dots altogether on this line. Next, make a dot on the left edge of the felt and 3 inches down from the top edge. Continue making dots every 3 inches along this line until you get to the right edge of the felt. Make a dot on the right edge as well. You'll make seven dots altogether along this line.

CONTINUED

5. Use the pencil and ruler to connect the dots. Begin at the left edge of the felt. Draw a line from the dot on the left edge up to the first dot on the top edge, then back down to the next dot, and so on. End by drawing a line from the last dot on the top edge to the dot on the right edge. Cut out the triangles with the scissors.

6. Use the hole punch to make two small holes on both the left and right sides of the felt. Make one hole about ½ inch in from the side and up from the bottom edge, and the other hole ½ inch from the side and 2½ inches up from the bottom edge.

7. Cut a piece of ribbon about 24 inches long. Poke the ribbon through the bottom-left hole and pull it through about halfway. Pick up the felt and form it into a crown, then thread one end of the ribbon through the bottom-right hole so that it mirrors the left side.

8. Crisscross the ribbons like you would a shoelace, taking the ribbon from the right side up to the top-left hole and the ribbon from the left side up to the top-right hole. Poke the ribbons through the holes, and tie them in a nice bow in the center. The laces can be loosened and tightened as needed to fit the owner's head.

9. Tie a small knot in both ends of the ribbon to prevent fraying.

Acknowledgments

THERE ARE SO MANY PEOPLE who have had a hand in shaping this book. Thank you to my editor, Hannah Elnan, and everyone at Sasquatch Books for making this experience a delightful one. Deepest thanks to both my agents, Mackenzie Brady and Danielle Barthel at New Leaf Literary, for believing so fully in me and in this project from day one. Their enthusiasm gave me confidence every step of the way.

Thank you to my photographer, Charity Burggraaf; my stylists, Renée Beaudoin and Shannon Douglas; and my designer, Anna Goldstein, for making this book more beautiful than I ever imagined. I owe a huge debt of gratitude to Andrea Smith, my illustrator. When I first saw her stunning artwork, before I'd even finished my book proposal, I knew it perfectly captured the essence of my book. I'm so thrilled to have her illustrations grace the pages of *Scandinavian Gatherings*.

I'm grateful for friends who allowed me to put their recipes in this book: thank you, Tania, Christina, and Marcelle. Thank you to Maria Stordahl Nelson of *Pink Patisserie* (PinkPatisserie.net) for being a great source of Scandinavian inspiration. Her blog is full of delicious Scandinavian recipes and beautiful photos. Thanks to Eva Jorgensen of Sycamore Street Press (SycamoreStreetPress.com) for being a longtime friend and a champion of this project.

I couldn't have written *Scandinavian Gatherings* without the help of an army of readers and testers: Caroline, Devon, Veeda, Sara, Amy A., Bre, Hannah, Linda A., Annie, P. J., Amy W., Marcelle, Haeley, Cyd, Amy C., Julie, Kristy, Laurel, Heidi, Brooke, Kim,

M. J., Marlene, Rachel, Sarah, Stephanie, my mother-in-law, my mom, and my sister, Emily. And to Katie H., Katie L., and Linda W., who collectively tested a dozen recipes for me at the last minute as I was scrambling to finish on time, a huge thank-you and a big hug!

Thanks to everyone who helped watch my kids while I wrote or cooked or made things. I have the most wonderful family and friends, and am constantly humbled by their generosity. Thank you, Mom, Dad, Chaz and family, Holly, Emily and family, Anna, Nana and Poppy—the best family a girl could ask for. I feel truly blessed to have a husband and kids who are always cheering me on, who happily go along with my dreams and schemes, no matter how crazy, and who don't mind a dining room table covered with skeins of yarn and bottle after bottle after bottle of craft paint. I love you, Speedy, Addie, Ellie, James, and George. To the moon and back.

And to Poppy, my darling grandpa, who inspired me to write this book in the first place, thank you, thank you, thank you.

Resources

SCANDINAVIAN INGREDIENTS

INGREDIENTS COMMON IN SCANDINAVIAN BAKING, such as pearl sugar or elderflower syrup, can be a bit of a challenge to find in your neighborhood grocery store. Shops like Ikea and World Market that carry goods from around the world are great places to check. We also found many ingredients for this book at Whole Foods and local Seattle stores like Metropolitan Market and Town & Country Markets. If you still can't find the ingredients you're looking for, Amazon usually has nearly everything.

Baking:

DANISH RYE BREAD: Copenhagen Pastry, RyeBreads.com

LINGONBERRY JAM: Whole Foods, WholeFoods.com; Ikea, Ikea.com

PEARL SUGAR: King Arthur Flour, KingArthurFlour.com; Sur La Table, SurLaTable.com

SCANDINAVIAN BAKING SUPPLIES: Ingebretsen's, Ingebretsens.com; Marina Market, MarinaMarket.com; Scandinavian Specialties, ScanSpecialties.com

Seafood:

LOX: Gerard & Dominique Seafoods, GDSeafoods.com

SALMON AND SMOKED SALMON: Loki Fish Co., LokiFish.com; Alaska Gold Brand Seafood Co-op, AlaskaGoldBrand.com

SCANDINAVIAN CRAFT SUPPLIES

Some of my go-to craft stores are Michaels and Jo-Ann. I also buy lots of harder-to-find supplies online through Amazon. Here is a list of specific supplies used in some of the crafts in this book:

STENCILED SWEDISH DALA HORSE NAPKINS: Tulip Soft Matte Fabric Paint in True Red, White, Petal Pink, Golden Yellow, and Cornflower (lightened by mixing it with some white paint)

DANISH TOWNHOUSE PLACE CARD HOLDERS: Martha Stewart Crafts Multi-Surface Satin Acrylic Craft Paint in Love Bird (red), Poodle Skirt (pink), Couscous (yellow), Wedding Cake (white), and Arrowhead (dark gray); DecoArt Americana Multi-Surface Satin Acrylic Paint in Paprika (terra-cotta); FolkArt Multi-Surface Satin Acrylic Paint in Sky Mist (light blue); Craft Smart Multi-Surface Premium Satin Acrylic Paint in Tangerine (mixed with white to make pale orange)

RUSTIC WELCOME SIGN: FolkArt Multi-Surface Satin Acrylic Craft Paint in Sky Mist

WOODLAND FELT GARLAND: Wool-blend felt from Prairie Point Junction in Bright Red, White, Camel, Moss, and Grassy Meadow

NO-SEW INLAID FELT COASTERS: Wool-blend felt from Benzie Design in Strawberry, White, and Icicle

FLORAL FOLK-ART SERVING TRAY: Design Master Colortool Spray Paint in Blue Sky; Martha Stewart Crafts Multi-Surface Satin Acrylic Craft Paint in Love Bird (red), Wedding Cake (white), Wild Blueberry (dark blue), Greek Tile (light blue), Fuchsia (dark pink), Poodle Skirt (pink), Putty (tan), Marmalade (orange), and Scottish Highlands (dark green)

HANGING PAPER FAN DECORATIONS: Paper Source (many different papers will work)

PAINTED FLAG PLACE MATS: DecoArt SoSoft Fabric Acrylics in Santa Red, Ultra White, and Navy Blue

PAINT-DIPPED PINECONE GARLAND: Martha Stewart Crafts Multi-Surface Satin Acrylic Craft Paint in Wedding Cake (white)

CANDLELIT EVERGREEN LUCIA TABLE WREATH: Rust-Oleum Painter's Touch Ultra Cover Paint + Primer in Hunt Club Green Satin

COLORFUL COOKIE PEDESTALS: Krylon ColorMaster Gloss Spray Paint in Banner Red, Blue Ocean Breeze, and Ballet Slipper (pink)

HAND-STAMPED WRAPPING PAPER: Martha Stewart Crafts Multi-Surface Satin Acrylic Craft Paint in Habanero (red), Wedding Cake (white), Scottish Highlands (dark green), and Spring Pasture (light green)

FELT BIRTHDAY CROWNS: Wool-blend felt from Benzie Design in Ochre and Icicle

SCANDINAVIAN HOME GOODS

Although several of the props in the book are vintage or family heirlooms, you can find many of them at the following stores.

GENERAL SCANDINAVIAN-INSPIRED HOME GOODS:

- Anthropologie, Anthropologie.com

- Crate and Barrel, CrateAndBarrel.com

- Ikea, Ikea.com

- Scandinavian Design Center, ScandinavianDesignCenter.com

- Terrain (Westport, CT), ShopTerrain.com

- The Nordic Maid (Poulsbo, WA), NordicMaid.com

- West Elm, WestElm.com

- Williams-Sonoma, Williams-Sonoma.com

BAKEWARE:

- Nordic Ware, NordicWare.com

CERAMICS:

- Speck and Stone, SpeckAndStone.com

- FiftyOneAndaHalf Ceramics, FiftyOneAndAHalf.com

- Akiko's Pottery, AkikosPottery.com

SCANDINAVIAN CULTURE

SCANDINAVIAN FESTIVAL (JUNCTION CITY, OR): This little town near us has a Scandinavian festival every August. The festival has authentic folk dancing, costumes, and food. ScandinavianFestival.com

POULSBO, WA: A truly Scandinavian downtown with a lot of festivals (its official title is "Poulsbo: A Viking City"), along with the smaller, neighboring city of Scandia. If you need something specific (a mold, baked goods, dishware, linens, holiday decorations, etcetera), or are just looking for a Scandinavian experience, this is a good town to hit. Poulsbo is truly devoted to Scandinavia and is decorated all of the time. It's situated on Liberty Bay with lots of seafood restaurants along the water and marina. Recommended stores include Marina Market, Sluy's Bakery (for baked goods, doughs, and starters) and The Nordic Maid. CityofPoulsbo.com

BLOGS AND WEBSITES FOR SCANDINAVIAN STYLE AND FOOD

SWEET PAUL: SweetPaulMag.com

LITTLE SCANDINAVIAN: LittleScandinavian.com

CALL ME CUPCAKE: CallMeCupcake.se

PINK PATISSERIE: PinkPatisserie.net

Craft Templates

◦⟩⟩⟩✪⟨⟨⟨◦ ◦⟩⟩⟩✪⟨⟨⟨◦ ◦⟩⟩⟩✪⟨⟨⟨◦

To download and print the templates online, visit LuluTheBaker.com/Book/Templates

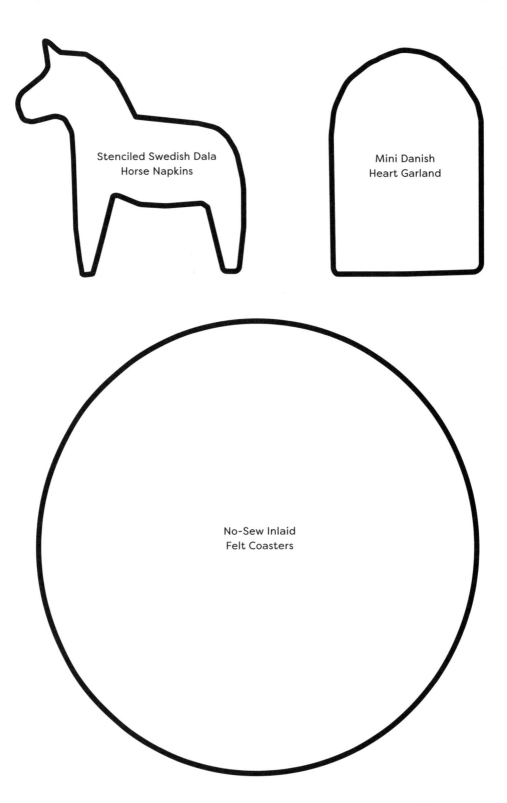

Stenciled Swedish Dala
Horse Napkins

Mini Danish
Heart Garland

No-Sew Inlaid
Felt Coasters

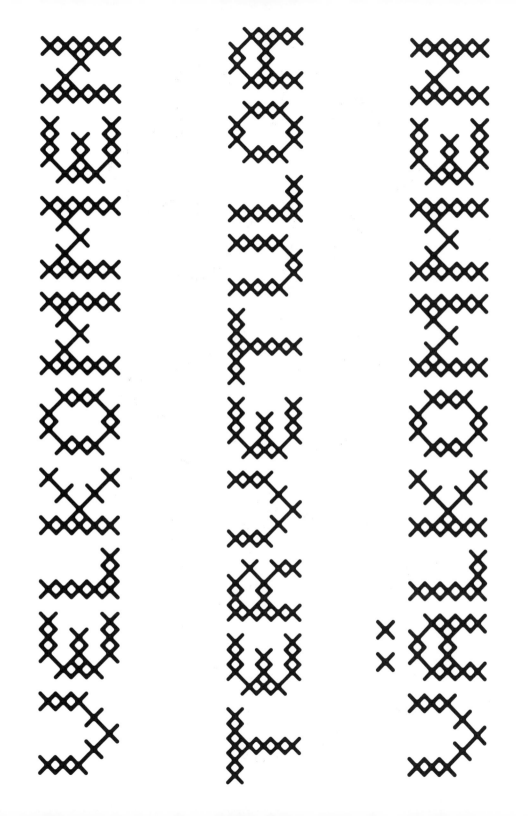

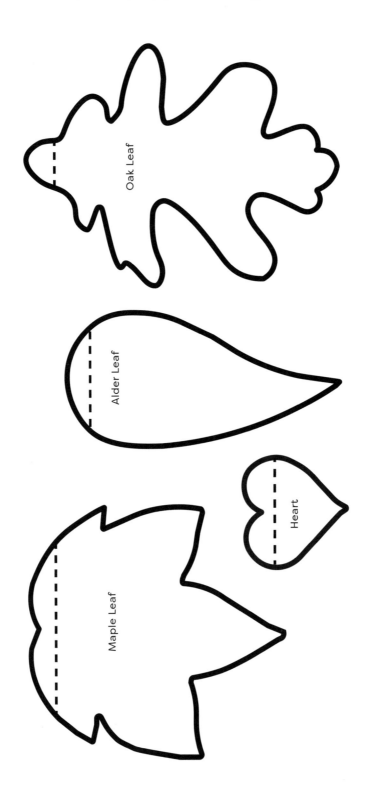

Oak Leaf

Alder Leaf

Heart

Maple Leaf

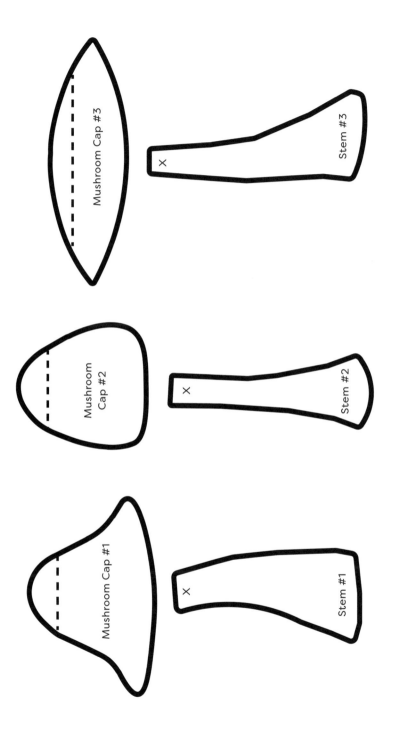

Mushroom Cap #3

Stem #3

X

Mushroom Cap #2

Stem #2

X

Mushroom Cap #1

Stem #1

X

Reduce or enlarge the template to fit your tray.

4"

6"

Index

‑›})‑❂{{‹‑ ‑›})‑❂{{‹‑ ‑›})‑❂{{‹‑

Note: Photographs are indicated by *italics*.

Conversions

VOLUME			LENGTH		WEIGHT	
UNITED STATES	METRIC	IMPERIAL	UNITED STATES	METRIC	AVOIRDUPOIS	METRIC
¼ tsp.	1.25 ml		⅛ in.	3 mm	¼ oz.	7 g
½ tsp.	2.5 ml		¼ in.	6 mm	½ oz.	15 g
1 tsp.	5 ml		½ in.	1.25 cm	1 oz.	30 g
½ Tbsp.	7.5 ml		1 in.	2.5 cm	2 oz.	60 g
1 Tbsp.	15 ml		1 ft.	30 cm	3 oz.	90 g
⅛ c.	30 ml	1 fl. oz.			4 oz.	115 g
¼ c.	60 ml	2 fl. oz.			5 oz.	150 g
⅓ c.	80 ml	2.5 fl. oz.			6 oz.	175 g
½ c.	125 ml	4 fl. oz.			7 oz.	200 g
1 c.	250 ml	8 fl. oz.			8 oz. (½ lb.)	225 g
2 c. (1 pt.)	500 ml	16 fl. oz.			9 oz.	250 g
1 qt.	1 l	32 fl. oz.			10 oz.	300 g

TEMPERATURE				11 oz.	325 g
OVEN MARK	FAHRENHEIT	CELSIUS	GAS	12 oz.	350 g
Very cool	250–275	130–140	½–1	13 oz.	375 g
Cool	300	150	2	14 oz.	400 g
Warm	325	165	3	15 oz.	425 g
Moderate	350	175	4	16 oz. (1 lb.)	450 g
Moderately hot	375	190	5	1½ lb.	750 g
	400	200	6	2 lb.	900 g
Hot	425	220	7	2¼ lb.	1 kg
	450	230	8	3 lb.	1.4 kg
Very Hot	475	245	9	4 lb.	1.8 kg

Printed in China

SASQUATCH BOOKS with colophon is a registered trademark of
Penguin Random House LLC

Originally published in hardcover in China
by Sasquatch Books in 2016.

27 26 25 24 23   9 8 7 6 5 4 3 2 1

Editor: Hannah Elnan | Production editor: Em Gale
Designer: Anna Goldstein | Photographs: Charity Burggraaf
Process photographs: Melissa Bahen | Illustrations: Andrea Smith
Map: Kat Marshello | Food Styling: Shannon Douglas
Prop styling and flowers: Renée Beaudoin
Copyeditor: Kristin Vorce Duran

Library of Congress Cataloging-in-Publication Data is available.

ISBN: 978-1-63217-499-4

Sasquatch Books
1325 Fourth Avenue, Suite 1025
Seattle, WA 98101

SasquatchBooks.com

MIX
Paper | Supporting
responsible forestry
FSC® C008047
FSC
www.fsc.org